The Homework Series

English A9

Malcolm Young

Published by Solomon Press
Marathas House, 11 Beech Hill,
Wellington, Somerset, TA21 8ER
Tel: 0700 900 1548
Email: info@solomon-press.com

Web site: www.solomon-press.com

The Homework Series is a trade mark of Solomon Press

© Malcolm Young 1999
First published 1999
First reprint 1999

ISBN 1-901724-08-5

All rights reserved
No part of this publication may be reproduced,
stored in a retrieval system, or transmitted in
any form or by any means without the prior
written permission of Solomon Press

Design and typesetting by Starturn Graphics, Sittingbourne, Kent.
Printed in the UK by The Short Run Press, Exeter, Devon.

Contents

Grammar

G1	Nouns	4
G2	Seven types of Pronoun	5
G3	Adjectives	7
G4	More practice with Adjectives	8
G5	Practice with Verbs	9
G6	Verbs - The Perfect Tenses	10
G7	Adverbs	11
G8	Prepositions	12
G9	Conjunctions	13

Punctuation

P1	Twelve uses of the Comma	14
P2	Punctuation practice	16
P3	Letters, Direct and Reported Speech	17

Spelling

S1	Easily confused words	18
S2	Frequently mis-spelt words	19

Figures of Speech and Literary Devices

F1	Similes, Metaphors, Personification	20
F2	Revision + Doubles and Palindromes	21
F3	Hyperbole, Litotes, Euphemism	22
F4	Malapropisms and Spoonerisms	23
F5	Limerick, Haiku, Clerihew	24

Comprehension Papers

In preparation for SATs Paper 1.

'Anne of Green Gables'	25
C1 and **C2**	27
'Brookstone School'	28
C3, **C4** and **C5**	29
'Hopi's Story'	30
C6 and **C7**	32
'Destruction of Planet Earth'	33
C8, **C9** and **C10**	34
'The Myrtle and the Ivy'	35
C11 and **C12**	37
Two poems about War	38
C13, **C14** and **C15**	39
'Shirley Vane'	40
C16 and **C17**	42
'Holiday Brochure'	43
C18, **C19** and **C20**	44
'A Wet Tuesday'	45
C21 and **C22**	47
'Animal Rescue Centre'	48
C23, **C24** and **C25**	49
'Oliver Runs Away'	50
C26 and **C27**	52
'Homelessness'	53
C28, **C29** and **C30**	54

Braintrains

B1	Treasure Hunt	55
B2	Crossword	56

GRAMMAR

Homeworks G1 to *G9* focus on the seven principal parts of speech: nouns, pronouns, adjectives, verbs, adverbs, conjunctions and prepositions. The work also touches on the lesser parts of speech: interjections and the articles.

HOMEWORK G1 — NOUNS

1 This passage contains 52 nouns.
Sort them into two lists: 26 **common nouns** and 26 **proper nouns**.

> 'Romeo and Juliet' is a tragedy by Shakespeare. It tells the story of two powerful families, the Montagues and the Capulets who lived in Verona, in Italy. They were deadly enemies, frequently getting into fights in the streets of the city, until the Prince threatened that the next person to break the peace would pay with his life. Romeo, only son of Montague, meets Juliet, only daughter of Capulet, at a masked ball and they fall in love. With the help of Juliet's nurse and a priest, Friar Laurence, they are married in secret. The same day a fight breaks out between Romeo's friend, Mercutio and Juliet's cousin, Tybalt. Romeo tries to stop them but in doing so Mercutio is killed. Romeo flies into a rage and kills Tybalt and for this Prince Escalus banishes him. The fateful events which follow for the two young lovers create one of Shakespeare's greatest romantic plays.

2 What is the **collective noun** for each of these groups?

governors   books   soldiers   bees
hounds   fish   trees   players

(and four difficult groups of birds)

gulls   partridges   snipe   choughs

3 Sort these nouns into four lists by gender: **masculine**, **feminine**, **common**, **neuter**.

stallion, widow, grief, choir, governess, son, peacock, computer, hen, cook, tea, bridegroom, duchess, actress, France, bachelor, squaw, prisoner, footballer, king, aunt, bluebell, landlord, dancer, baron, priest, waiter, hostess, sergeant, furniture, librarian, writer, pyjamas, tree, spinster, door, ship, nephew, vixen, model.

4 Which of these nouns are **countable** (*a* ... , *an* ... or a number) and which are **uncountable nouns** (*some* ...) ?

peach, flour, water, egg, bread, leaf, information, help, car, traffic, rain, sugar, weather.

5 Turn these adjectives into **abstract nouns**.

anxious, beautiful, sympathetic, painful, dangerous,
happy, religious, artistic, scientific, poor, stupid, just.

HOMEWORK G2 — SEVEN TYPES OF PRONOUN

This table serves as a reminder of the various types of pronoun.
Study it carefully and try to complete the exercises without referring to it.
If you are successful then you know all that there is to know about pronouns.

	1(s)	2(s)	3(s)	3(s)	3(s)	1(pl)	2(pl)	3(pl)
Personal (Subject):	I	you	he	she	it	we	you (pl)	they
Personal (Object):	me	you	him	her	it	us	you	them
Possessive Pronoun	mine	yours	his	hers	its	ours	yours	theirs
Reflexive Pronoun:	myself	yourself	himself	herself	itself	ourselves	yourselves	themselves

Interrogative pronouns: stand in for nouns in questions: *who? whom? whose? which? what?*

Indefinite pronouns: take the place of unspecified persons, places or things: *one, none, any, other, some, each, either, neither, few, several, no-one, nobody, everybody, somebody, anybody, much, more, most.*

Relative pronouns: *who, whom, whose, which, that.*

Demonstrative pronouns: *this, that, these, those.*

1 Insert **personal pronouns**, **subject** or **object form** into each sentence.

   a We often visited .... (3pl) but they never came to see .... (1pl).
   b When .... (2s) met .... (3s) did she recognise ...., (2s)?
   c He can jump higher than .... (3s) but she can run faster than .... (3s).
   d That card was from .... (1s) but .... (3pl) thought it was from .... (2s).

2 Rewrite these sentences without any reference to gender.

   a Each member of the band is responsible for his own instrument.
   b If an inspector spots a mistake, he must report it at once.
   c An applicant must apply himself or he will be disqualified.
   d Each passenger must look after his own passport.

3 Insert *I* or *me* into these sentences, changing the word order if needed.

   a .... and Harry used to be the best of friends.
   b You and .... and Sheila will represent the school.
   c It was a draw so the cup was shared by George and ....
   d The letter was addressed to Susan, ... and Sharon.

continued …

HOMEWORK G2 CONTINUED

4 Insert **reflexive pronouns** into each sentence.

   a She is going to buy … a new skirt.
   b You can be very proud of … .
   c The original cast will be appearing … .
   d I told … that I could do it.

5 Rewrite each sentence, using **possessive pronouns** instead of nouns to avoid repetition.

   a She said the book was *her book* but I knew that it was *my book*.
   b I said, "Are you sure it is *your book*?"
   c John complicated matters by saying that it was *his book*.
   d Having been told to go to our rooms, we went to *our rooms* and they went to *their rooms*.

6 Insert **interrogative pronouns** into each sentence.

   a … is taking you and with … are you going to stay?
   b … are those suitcases and … are these?
   c … is your favourite television programme?
   d … of these two colours do you prefer?

7 These sentences, using **indefinite pronouns**, contain errors of agreement.
Rewrite each one correctly, underlining the words you have corrected.

   a None of the walkers have been seen since ten o'clock this morning.
   b Every one of the forty passengers were rescued before the boat sank.
   c One can only be expected to do his or her best.
   d Each of the seven teams have to play four games in the first round.

8 Use **relative pronouns** to join each of these pairs of sentences into one.

   a This is my cousin Sean. He lives in Dublin.
   b Mary is a hotel inspector. Her work takes her all over the country.
   c There is the house. It was once lived in by Charles Dickens.
   d Mrs Fry is leaving on Friday. We are buying a present for her.

9 From these sentences identify all fourteen pronouns.
State which of the seven types each one is.

   a I went to see my aunt but she was out so I missed her.
   b David said to himself, "What shall I have for dinner?"
   c "This is serious," the policeman said. "Who was here last night?"
   d My friend, with whom I was staying, said no-one had been there.
   e Carol herself admitted, "These are not mine."

HOMEWORK G3 — ADJECTIVES

1 Pick out the 25 descriptive adjectives used in this passage from "Moby Dick" by Herman Melville to describe the sighting of the great whale.

"At length the breathless hunter came so nigh his seemingly unsuspecting prey, that his entire dazzling hump was distinctly visible, sliding along the sea, as if an isolated thing, and continually set in a revolving ring of finest, fleecy, greenish foam. He saw the vast, involved wrinkles of the slightly projecting head beyond. Before it, far out on the soft Turkish-rugged waters, went the glistening white shadow from his broad, milky forehead, a musical rippling playfully accompanying the shade; and behind, the blue waters interchangeably flowed over into the moving valley of his steady wake; and on either hand bright bubbles arose and danced by his side."

2 Melville used 25 adjectives in a passage of just over 100 words.
How does that compare with your own use?
Find a piece of your own descriptive writing and count the number of adjectives.

> **YOU NEED TO KNOW ...**
>
> *my, your, his, her, its, our, their* are **possessive adjectives** when they are used with a noun.

3 Seven of the following sentences contain **possessive adjectives** and three do not.
Sort them out.

- **a** Is this your house?
- **b** Susie took me to see her cat.
- **c** I finished my homework in an hour.
- **d** Their train was very late.
- **e** The police found her quite soon.
- **f** It's going to be a hot summer.
- **g** Our team was the clear winner.
- **h** I entered my picture in the competition.
- **i** We all knew the ball was his.
- **j** Her aunt was her legal guardian.

4 Choose from the endings *-ful, -ic, -ern, -ous, -al, -ish, -ing,* or *-y* to make adjectives from the following nouns.

child, west, care, hero, danger, fool, fame, skeleton, religion, loyalty, interest, north, centre, summer, victory, faith, autumn, baby, voice, music, shadow, metre, anxiety, nose, giant.

5 Change these proper nouns into adjectives, remembering to keep the capital letters.

Ireland, Victoria, Napoleon, Scotland, Wales, Britain, Japan, Manchester, Liverpool, Cornwall, Shakespeare, Shaw.

HOMEWORK G4 — MORE PRACTICE WITH ADJECTIVES

1 Remembering the accepted order of adjectives (**opinion - size - age - shape - colour - origin - material - purpose**) insert the adjectives into these sentences.

a I went on a ……, ……, …… journey. (*sight-seeing, short, fascinating*)
b Mary was wearing a ……, ……, ……, …… coat. (*sheepskin, peculiar, Chinese, old*)
c He was driving a ……, ……, …… car. (*black, American, huge*)
d He gave her a pair of ……, ……, ……, …… earrings. (*amethyst, beautiful, antique, purple*)
e They lived in a ……, ……, ……, ……, …… cottage. (*old, lonely, little, farm, Scottish.*)
f We bought a ……, ……, ……, ……, ……, ……, ……, …… table. (*eighteenth-century, oval, oak, delightful, dining, enormous, French, black*).

2 Form adjectives from these verbs.

invent, invite, ride, write, eat, freeze, speak, tear, weave, obey, swell, steal.

> You will remember that the **interrogative pronouns** *whose? which? what?* are not followed by a noun or pronoun whereas when the same words are **interrogative adjectives** they are.

3 Insert the appropriate **interrogative adjective** into each of these sentences.

a … colour are you painting the walls?
b … coat is this?
c … tie do you prefer?

4 Adjectives ending in *-ing* usually describe what something is like, whereas adjectives ending in *-ed* usually describe people's feelings.
Insert the correct adjectives into these sentences.

a The book had an …… ending. The class was …… about the trip. (*exciting/excited*)
b We found the talk ……. We were …… in what he had to say. (*interesting/interested*)
c The children were …… by the clowns. It was a most …… programme. (*amusing/amused*)
d They were very …… people. It was a …… holiday. (*disappointing/disappointed*)

5 Copy this passage and insert the 25 missing adjectives.
Do not use the same adjective twice.

The sky was …… and …… and a ……, …… wind blew as we left the …… harbour. Soon …… waves began to break over the ……, …… boat and even …… Jack wore a …… expression on his usually …… face. Once out of the lee of the …… island the …… force of the …… gale hit us, screaming in the …… sails and rigging. …… Emily huddled in a corner, her …… eyes looking even more …… as the ……, …… rain slashed against her …… face. The …… sky and the …… sea seemed to merge into a …… whole carrying our …… craft where it would.

HOMEWORK G5 — PRACTICE WITH VERBS

1. List the 21 verbs in this passage.

> 'Nick listened but the only sound was the odd droplet of water which dripped from the roof and echoed in the vast emptiness of the cave. He had been lost for what seemed like hours and he knew that the batteries in his torch would not last much longer. The light had flickered and dimmed and so he had switched the torch off. Once more he shouted but in the darkness the sound of his voice only intensified the loneliness he felt. "They will come," he told himself. "They will be looking for me, I know." He was feeling cold and tired but he knew that he must not sleep.'

2. These sentences contain errors of agreement. Rewrite each one correctly.

   a. One of you two boys are in trouble.
   b. Fred and his sister is going to the party too.
   c. The Regiment of soldiers are back.
   d. Where is my shirt and my shorts?

3. Change the number and person in these sentences as indicated in brackets.

   a. They are selling their car and their caravan.   (Change to 1st person plural.)
   b. I hope that I will pass my test.   (Change to 3rd person single, feminine.)
   c. The trees will soon have shed their leaves.   (Change to 3rd person singular.)
   d. Are you certain that you brought your case?   (Change to 3rd person plural.)
   e. He has been awarded his swimming certificate.   (Change to 2nd person plural.)

4. List the verbs used in the nine sentences in Questions 2 and 3 above, in their infinitive form.

5. This passage is written in the future simple tense. Rewrite it in the past simple tense.

> Tomorrow I will catch the train to Banbury and I will visit my old friend, Beryl. The journey will take about half an hour and I will walk the rest of the way. I will arrive in time for coffee and we will have plenty to talk about. I will take her out for lunch as I always do at The Singing Kettle. We will arrive there early because that way we will have the best choice, but Beryl will have fish and chips as she always does. I will be more adventurous and try their goulash. After lunch Beryl will walk down to the station and will wait with me until my train arrives to take me home again.

6. Write these sentences with the verbs in the tenses indicated.

   a. I (*to bring*) the boxes home with me. (past simple)
   b. She (*to sell*) her collection of ornaments. (present continuous)
   c. The various tribes (*to fight*) each other. (past continuous)
   d. Madame LeBonne (*to teach*) you French. (future continuous)
   e. You (*to sleep*) in the attic. (future simple)
   f. We (*to be*) the party from the school. (present simple)

7. Rewrite the six sentences from Question 6 in the negative form.

HOMEWORK G6 — VERBS - THE PERFECT TENSES

In Books "E7" and "E8" we looked at the three tenses of verbs - **past**, **present** and **future**, and went on to look at each of those in their **simple** and **continuous** forms.

EXAMPLE:
I walked (past simple tense)
I was walking (past continuous)
I walk (present simple)
I am walking (present continuous)
I will walk (future simple)
I will be walking (future continuous)

The perfect tense tells us about actions just completed in the past, present or future.

I had walked (past perfect) (sometimes called the **pluperfect**)
I have walked (present perfect)
I shall have walked (future perfect)

The **perfect continuous tense** tells us about actions which may be finished or not finished.

I had been walking (past perfect continuous) (or pluperfect continuous)
I have been walking (present perfect continuous)
I shall have been walking (future perfect continuous)

1 Rewrite each sentence using perfect tenses.

a Betty is training to fly gliders.
b We will travel to Scotland on Sunday.
c I wiped the dust from the old canoe.
d Julie is marrying John Anderson.
e They were not looking for us.
f Do you live in Manchester?

2 Now rewrite the six sentences above using perfect continuous tenses.

You will notice from Questions 1 and 2 that with regular verbs the present participle is formed by adding *-ing* to the infinitive. The past participle is formed by adding *-ed* to the infinitive. However, not all verbs are regular.

3 Complete these tables of irregular verbs.

Present	Past	Past Participle
give	gave	given
saw		
know		
freeze		
spring		
cut		
write		
swim		
shake		
rise		

Present	Past	Past Participle
drink		
speak		
ring		
throw		
hurt		
weave		
tread		
ride		
seek		
fight		

HOMEWORK G7 — ADVERBS

> REMEMBER THAT …
> An **adverb of manner** answers the question *How?*
> An **adverb of time** answers the question *When?*
> An **adverb of place** answers the question *Where?*

1 From this passage list the eleven **adverbs** or **adverbial phrases** of **manner**, five of **time** and eight of **place**.

The current flowed swiftly and relentlessly down the river, carrying our little raft here, there and everywhere. Then, suddenly, for a few seconds, we heard in the distance a strange roaring sound. Quickly I glanced at Tom, as I desperately tried to control the makeshift rudder. Seldom had I seen him so dreadfully pale, his eyes tightly closed. The current tossed us carelessly over the rapids and around the rocks and soon the roar was frighteningly louder. It was unmistakably the sound of the Great Falls and before long I could clearly see a curtain of mists and rainbows ahead.

> REMEMBER THAT …
> **Interrogative adverbs** are used to ask questions. (*How? Where? When? Why?*, …)
> **Relative adverbs** include the same words as interrogatives above but without asking questions they join clauses together.
> **Adverbs of Degree** answer the question How much? (*very, too, quite, almost, totally,* …)
> **Adverbs of Frequency** answer the question How often? (*always, never, sometimes, twice,* …)
> **Adverbs of Probability** tell us how sure we are about something. (*yes, no, perhaps, certainly*)

2 From these sentences list the adverbs and say what sort each is from the five kinds detailed above. (There may be more than one in a sentence.)

   a Where have you been and why did you not phone us?
   b Probably you will tell us when you have thought of a reason.
   c Julie was very confident after practising three times a day.
   d He ran too fast and was completely exhausted.
   e When were you going to say how you were always chosen to play?
   f Yes, I often wondered why you were only asked twice.

> It was once thought to be very poor English to **split the infinitive**. This is when an adverb is placed in the middle of the infinitive form of a verb. EXAMPLES: *to boldly go*, *to clearly see*. Nowadays the ruling on this is not so strict but it is as well to know that *to go boldly*, or *clearly to see* is still generally considered to be better.

3 Rewrite these sentences without split infinitives.

   a We hoped to eventually arrive before midnight.
   b The plumber tried to completely stop the leak and to finally mend the pipe.
   c To deliberately ignore the sign was very foolish.
   d They were allowed to happily play all day and to almost forget everything else.

HOMEWORK G8

PREPOSITIONS

1 Copy the passage below and insert the twenty **prepositions**.
round, to, towards, beside, behind, about, by, into, against, through, inside, across, after, beneath, opposite, down, from, among, at, along.

The stranger ran …… the road and …… the path …… the Bank. For a moment he was lost …… the crowds but then I spotted him hurrying …… the corner and …… a side-street. Going …… him I was in time to see him slipping …… a small cafe. Peering …… the window I saw him speaking to a girl …… the counter before sitting …… a table …… the wall. Once …… the cafe I looked …… casually, ordered a cup of tea …… the girl and took it …… a table …… the door. …… the table I aimed my camera …… the stranger …… me.

2 Complete these **idioms** by inserting the appropriate preposition and then say what you think each one means.

    a paying …… the nose   **b** clutching …… straws
    c have a shot …… something   **d** stick …… your guns
    e beating …… the bush   **f** straight …… the shoulder
    g thrown …… the scent   **h** put the cart …… the horse
    i going …… the grain   **j** laying …… the law

Compound prepositions (made up of more than one word) include: *with regard to, according to, by means of, in addition to, in front of, in spite of, due to, except for, instead of.*

3 Make up nine sentences using each of the compound prepositions listed above.

4 Certain words are usually followed by particular prepositions;
Rewrite these sentences, inserting the most suitable prepositions.

    a Her sister was suffering …… a bad cold. *(from / with)*
    b He refused to comment …… the reports in the paper. *(about / on)*
    c Her painting was excellent in comparison …… the rest of the entries. *(with / to)*
    d The castle was different …… all the others we had seen. *(than / from / to)*
    e The residents were ignorant …… the new road plan. *(about / of)*
    f You may divide the chocolate …… the six of you. *(among / between)*
    g I borrowed this bat …… my friend Cilla. *(off / from)*
    h We were very disappointed …… the film. *(in / with)*
    i Miss Cathcart was very angry …… us for making such a mess. *(at / with)*
    j They say that black is the opposite …… white. *(to / from / of)*

HOMEWORK G9 **CONJUNCTIONS**

In previous work we looked at conjunctions simply as words which we use to join together other words, phrases, clauses or simple sentences.
NOW YOU NEED TO KNOW ...
There are two kinds of conjunction: coordinators and subordinators.
Coordinating conjunctions join together units of equal status and include: *and, but, or, so, yet, or, as well as, for, neither ... nor, either ... or, both ... and.*
Subordinating conjunctions join subordinate or dependent clauses to the main clause of the sentence and include: *although, if, because, as, before, after, since, until, when, where, while, whereas, so that.*

1 Use a variety of **coordinating conjunctions** to join together these simple sentences.

   a I went shopping. I bought a C.D.
   b Louise ran down the road. Louise missed the bus.
   c Jack could go swimming. Jack could stay at home.
   d The visitor was not Max. The visitor was not Maria.
   e My aunt gave me a book. She also gave me a pen.
   f The weather forecast is for rain. The weather forecast is for sun.

2 Use a variety of **subordinating conjunctions** to join these together.

   a She was very sad ...... the film ended.
   b I felt quite ill ...... I had eaten.
   c ...... it rained quite a lot, we still enjoyed ourselves.
   d We all shouted for help ...... we thought we were lost.
   e ...... he is late, we will leave without him ...... he learns a lesson.
   f I would wait ...... she arrived ...... I am in a great hurry.

YOU NEED TO KNOW ...
Some words, such as *before, after, until, over, through, since, for,* can serve as **conjunctions**, **prepositions** or **adverbs**, depending on how they are used.
A conjunction introduces a clause, needing a subject and a verb. (I ate *before* I left home.)
A **preposition** is followed by a noun or pronoun. (This is the calm *before* the storm.)
An **adverb** relates to its verb. (I am sure I have been here *before*.)

3 In each sentence decide whether the words in italic are conjunctions, prepositions or adverbs.

   a *After* leaving him at the station, we have not seen him *since*.
   b He ran *over* the fields *until* he was out of sight.
   c Someone has been *through* this door *since* teatime *when* we closed it.
   d I have kept this *for* him *since* he left *but* now our friendship is *over*.
   e She arrived *before* him *and* waited *outside until* she saw his car.

PUNCTUATION

HOMEWORK P1 TWELVE USES OF THE COMMA

The comma is an extremely useful punctuation mark but is frequently misused. The exercises on these two pages cover all the main uses of the comma.

1 Lists. Use commas to separate the items listed in these sentences.

　a I went shopping and bought beans onions potatoes carrots and peas.
　b She was offered a choice of spaghetti on toast ravioli fish and chips or a baked potato.
　c We drove to Truro did some shopping had lunch went to the cinema and watched 'Titanic'.
　d History Geography French and English are my favourite subjects.

2 Use commas to separate lists of adjectives or adverbs remembering the OSASCOMP order: (opinion → size → age → shape → colour → origin → material → purpose).

　a She gave us a ghastly little old round red French earthenware cooking pot.
　b John was wearing a lovely new blue Italian wool sweater.
　c The travellers made their way home slowly wearily silently and sadly.
　d Children played innocently happily and noisily in the waves.

3 In these sentences commas are needed to separate the direct speech.

　a She said "I hope you will be very happy here."
　b "This is the workroom" Betty explained "where we make the soft toys."
　c "Thank you for all you have done for us" he replied.
　d "I am leaving now" Brian shouted "and I shan't be back until late."

4 Use commas to separate the names of people being addressed in these sentences.

　a Please Rupert don't sit on my desk.
　b Mr Jones the sergeant will see you now.
　c I have been waiting for you for an hour Harriet.
　d Ladies and Gentlemen please welcome The Flying Flanagans.

5 In a similar way use commas to separate question phrases.

　a You did remember the picnic didn't you?
　b You will have another cup won't you before you leave?
　c It's a wonderful day today isn't it?
　d Ruth and Ray have arrived haven't they?

6 Certain words and phrases like *yes, however, no doubt, meanwhile* need to be separated from the rest of the sentence.

　a No you may not have another pair of trainers.
　b We are hoping therefore to hear no more about it.
　c Finally we are hoping to spend a couple of days at Disneyworld.

continued …

14

HOMEWORK P1 CONTINUED

7 Use commas to separate additional clauses which are not absolutely necessary.

   a Jack who is a lorry driver gave me a lift to Manchester.
   b I am waiting for Mr Shaw my wife's father and Miss Rowland my cousin.
   c Edinburgh the Athens of the North is a very beautiful city.
   d Elsie hurrying to catch the train forgot her briefcase.
   e Dressed entirely in red the bride surprised everyone.

8 Commas may be necessary to avoid ambiguity.
Write each sentence twice, with the comma in a different place to change the meaning.

   a In June I shall be on holiday perhaps with Sidney.
   b Opposite the house was a magnificent sight.
   c Outside the field was a mass of yellow daffodils.

9 Use commas in these numbers to separate millions, thousands and hundreds.

   a 14563108   **b** 346709764   **c** 1657301

10 Use commas here to separate day of the week from date and the month from the year.

   a Tuesday 2nd. July 1941   **b** Saturday 1st. January 2000

11 In this simple letter 8 commas may be used and 5 full stops should be used.
Rewrite it, inserting commas and full stops.

> 23 Sycamore Street
> Forest Park
> Nottingham
> NH23 6RH
>
> Wednesday 14th March 2001
>
> Dear Mr Monroe
>
> Thank you for the invitation which I will reply to shortly
>
> Yours sincerely
>
> R Hood

12 Commas are needed when two parts of a sentence are inverted.
Invert these sentences and insert the necessary commas.

   a You will all be expected to attend unless you have a really good excuse.
   b The class continued to jeer in spite of being told to be quiet.
   c We did not get there in time because the car broke down.
   d They were perfectly contented until they saw what they had missed.

HOMEWORK P2 — PUNCTUATION PRACTICE

1 Commas have been left out of these sentences.
Rewrite each one correctly with commas.

  a We were able to find A B C and D but not E F or G.
  b He smiled in a kind sympathetic way and when he spoke his voice was soft deep and soothing.
  c I shook him slapped him shouted at him and even kicked him but still he would not move.
  d The tiger inched closer slowly quietly dangerously.
  e Waiting watching she tried not to move not to breathe.
  f The Kraken awoke an enormous strange terrifying creature.
  g My friends Becky Tina Kylie and Rosie came to visit me in hospital.
  h Becky a florist brought me flowers pink yellow and white roses.
  i "I'm afraid" he said "your bag books lunch and P.E. kit have all disappeared."
  j "You will try to visit me won't you?" she said tears brimming in her eyes.

2 Apostrophes have been left out of these sentences.
Rewrite each one correctly.

  a Its eight oclock already and Im sure Ive forgotten something.
  b I dont know what time theyre arriving but theyll probably be late.
  c Julies hoping shes been picked for the team but it isnt likely.
  d Were wondering why we cant see whats stopping its wheels going round.
  e Harrys mother collected the childrens toys for the Schools bazaar.
  f Mrs Jones class had to wait while she fetched the key of the girls changing room.
  g James uncle painted all the houses front doors apart from Number Fives.
  h Freds dogs hurt its paw which is why its whining.

3 In these sentence you need to insert inverted commas, double for speech and quotations, single for titles and so on.

  a Mrs Wogan announced, The tickets have arrived for our holiday.
  b We leave on a Sunday, she said, and return the following Saturday.
  c What time does the plane leave? Katie asked.
  d It leaves at two oclock in the afternoon, she replied. Any other questions?
  e This is the house. It has four bedrooms. Would you like to go in? she enquired.
  f On Monday we are going to see Peter Pan at the Grand Theatre, Mark told them.
  g Louise read out, It says in The South Wales Echo, This is a spectacular production.
  h Who said, A horse, a horse! My kingdom for a horse!? the questionmaster asked.
  i The next question was, In Hamlet what is the name of the father of Hamlet?
  j Jane asked, Who wrote, Shall I compare thee to a summer's day??

HOMEWORK P3 — LETTERS, DIRECT AND REPORTED SPEECH

1 Set out this letter, using full punctuation.

23 cornhill avenue hinchcliffe gloucester ba23 8dg 23rd march 1999 from mr d g holmes warburton and pearce 42 to 48 north parade overton west sussex br4 9pt to dear mr holmes thank you for your letter of 2nd march regarding the room ventilator which my wife and i bought from your company in february i am sorry to have taken so long to reply to your letter you will doubtless recall that when the ventilator arrived i wrote to inform you that we could not get it to work in your reply you suggested that we return the machine to you for inspection since then my grandson has been to visit us and he discovered that the reason why it would not work was because there were no batteries in it there was no mention of batteries in your original advertisement anyway it worked quite well for a fortnight but now the batteries have run out does this mean i have to spend £2.49 on batteries every two weeks we are old age pensioners and cant afford this what are you going to do about this yours sincerely donald b foster

2 Rewrite these sentences as reported speech.
EXAMPLE: *John said, "I will not be there."* becomes *John said that he would not be there.*

a "I am extremely pleased to meet you, Mrs Yard," Nicholas said, smiling.
b Mrs Yard replied, "The pleasure is mine. I have wanted to visit you for a long time."
c "We will leave at 9.30 tomorrow," Jane announced. "Do not forget."
d "Where are my library books?" Ellen asked. "I am going to be late for school."
e "Take care that you don't fall," Jill warned, "or you will spill the water."
f "I assure you that 'To be or not to be' comes from 'Hamlet'", Mr Harris insisted.

3 Rewrite this extract from a play as direct speech.
Use inverted commas, paragraphs and avoid the word *said*.

Brad:	Don't make so much noise. I know the house is empty but we still need to be quiet.
Minty:	It's O.K. Don't worry. I haven't broken my leg. I'm not bleeding to death.
Sol:	Where's the light switch?
Brad:	Don't put the light on, you idiot!
Sol:	But I can't see.
Brad:	Just wait a minute. Your eyes will soon adjust to the darkness.
Minty:	Shsh! Listen?
Brad:	What is it?
Minty:	I thought I heard something. Yes! There it is again. There's somebody walking about upstairs.
Sol:	I'm out of here. I said we shouldn't have come in the first place.
Brad:	Stay where you are, and be quiet! Whoever it is is coming down the stairs. If we go through the hall they'll see us. Hide behind those curtains. Quickly!

SPELLING

HOMEWORK S1   **SPELLING - CONFUSED WORDS**

1. This question deals with **synonyms** - words with similar meanings. However, no two words have exactly the same meaning. Write a sentence for each of these words to show that you understand the differences in their meanings.

    a   adjacent - adjoining
    b   protect - defend
    c   close - shut
    d   cease - stop
    e   admitted - confessed
    f   reward - award
    g   counterfeit - artificial
    h   strictly - severely
    i   famous - notorious
    j   frail - fragile
    k   accurate - correct
    l   forgery - fraud

2. This question includes words which have different meanings but are often confused. Write a sentence for each to show its meaning.

    a   astronomy - astrology
    b   corporal punishment - capital punishment
    c   malevolent - malignant
    d   enquiry - inquiry
    e   dominating - domineering
    f   crevasse - crevice
    g   eligible - illegible
    h   emigrate - immigrate
    i   compliment - complement
    j   urban - urbane
    k   poignant - pungent
    l   emancipated - emaciated

3. This set of words are **homonyms** (also called **homophones**). Write sentences for these words that sound alike but have different meanings.

    a   exercise - exorcise
    b   gorilla - guerrilla
    c   hail - hale
    d   holy - holey - wholly
    e   metal - mettle
    f   meter - metre
    g   navel - naval
    h   write - right - rite
    i   forgone - foregone
    j   flair - flare
    k   president - precedent
    l   draft - draught

4. This set of words includes some of the most frequently confused words in our language. Write a sentence for each word.

    a   cloths - clothes
    b   currant - current
    c   desert - dessert
    d   practice - practise
    e   principle - principal
    f   stationary - stationery
    g   accept - except
    h   older - elder
    i   lightening - lightning
    j   license - licence
    k   program - programme
    l   breathe - breath

HOMEWORK S2 — FREQUENTLY MIS-SPELT WORDS

The first eight lists revise words from Books *English A7* and *English A8*.
Lists 9 to 15 contain the words most frequently mis-spelt by Year 9 students.

Take each list, one at a time, learn it and then have a friend test you.
Each test can build in number and should include a few words from previous tests.

List 1
potatoes
outrageous
believable
receive
seize
ghastly
catarrh
rheumatism
illegible
irresistible

List 2
disappearance
independent
illegal
honourable
changeable
noticeable
instructor
endeavour
passenger
hygienic

List 3
spacious
slaughter
muscle
yacht
handkerchief
invisible
scientific
immaterial
behaviour
friendliness

List 4
replaceable
island
scissors
plumber
volcanoes
canoe
definitely
separate
dinosaur
procedure

List 5
houseful
computer
ceiling
carriage
correspondence
conscious
ascend
conqueror
column
innocent

List 6
actor
massacre
gracious
Christian
niece
cupboard
neighbour
benefited
forfeit
accommodation

List 7
jewellery
parallel
gardener
heiress
nuisance
playwright
instalment
deceitful
foreign
sincerely

List 8
literature
impatient
negligible
committee
calendar
autumn
paralysis
bicycle
humorous
diarrhoea

List 9
brilliant
author
business
knowledgeable
mosquito
criticism
government
parliament
unnecessary
cemetery

List 10
advertisement
bargain
campaign
pigeon
queue
extraordinary
raspberry
receipt
chauffeur
grammar

List 11
commemorate
apology
association
descendent
fascinating
refrigerator
thoroughly
syllabus
excitement
suspicious

List 12
argument
basically
mischievous
satellite
discipline
February
recommendation
height
occurrence
supervisor

List 13
aeroplane
biscuit
fulfil
miscellaneous
silhouette
embarrass
sergeant
raspberry
Mediterranean
physique

List 14
amateur
burglary
plateau
sceptre
psychology
forty
environment
susceptible
medieval
analysis

List 15
beautiful
laboratory
secretary
sovereign
tying
interruption
exaggeration
spherical
veterinary
miniature

FIGURES OF SPEECH - LITERARY DEVICES

HOMEWORK F1   **SIMILES, METAPHORS AND PERSONIFICATION**

1   Choose suitable **similes** to complete these sentences.

    a   The holiday traffic crawled like …
    b   Mrs Cross was as angry as …
    c   Like … the rain continued to fall.
    d   It was as hot as …, the sun beating down like …
    e   Feeling as tired as … Brian dawdled on his way to school like …
    f   The fire burned on like … , as … as … , devouring everything in its path like …

2   Complete these **similes** that have become so overused that they are in danger of becoming **cliches** and should be used sparingly in your writing.

    a   As fit as a …
    b   As flat as a …
    c   As heavy as …
    d   As happy as a …
    e   As keen as …
    f   As dead as a …
    g   As stubborn as a …
    h   As playful as a …
    i   As poor as a …
    j   As sharp as a …
    k   As blind as a …
    l   As pleased as …

3   With the twelve expressions from Question 2 write similes of your own.

4   Make up sentences using vivid comparisons in the form of **metaphors** to describe these:

    a   a rocky, dangerous shore
    b   a river in flood
    c   a huge ship docking
    d   clouds gathering on the horizon
    e   robots in a car factory
    f   a very dark and silent night
    g   a train entering a station
    h   shelves of books in a library

5   Create personification by giving each of these nouns a *humanising* adjective.

    a   mountain
    b   darkness
    c   water
    d   forest
    e   sky
    f   ship
    g   thorns
    h   storm

6   Use personification by adding humanising verbs or adverbs to these sentences.

    a   The traffic was grid-locked, and cars and lorries … (vb) and … (vb) at each other.
    b   Fierce brambles …(vb) … (adv) and … (adv) at the passing stranger.
    c   The lonely tree … (vb) and … (vb) … (adv) in the icy wind.
    d   Orchards of white marched … (adv) across the hills, … (adv) scattering their blossoms.
    e   An ominous thick fog … (vb) … (adv) into the hut and … (vb) secretly into each corner.

7   In these sentences list all the examples of **similes, metaphors** and **personification**.

    a   The telephone rang, crying out to be answered, a lonely voice in the empty house.
    b   Like an untiring mountaineer the little bird soared into the snowy mountains of the clouds.
    c   The storm hit the sleeping town like an avenging angel seeking out fresh victims.
    d   Huge pylons strode across the hills like invading giants.

HOMEWORK F2 — REVISION PLUS DOUBLES AND PALINDROMES

Write a definition for each of these terms.
In each case the term is followed by an example to help you.

1 **Alliteration**.
   EXAMPLE: "And weeds in wheels grow long and lovely and lush."

2 **Assonance**.
   EXAMPLE: "Down and around and the sound drowned out."

3 **Cliche**.
   EXAMPLE: A little bird told me that it was a matter of life and death.

4 **Colloquialism**.
   EXAMPLE: Pull your socks up and let's get cracking.

5 **Hyperbole**.
   EXAMPLE: I offered a thousand apologies.

6 **Onomatopoeia**.
   EXAMPLE: We heard ducks quacking, bees buzzing and the clattering of hooves.

7 **Proverb**.
   EXAMPLE: Early to bed, early to rise, makes a man healthy, wealthy and wise.

8 **Pun**.
   EXAMPLE: Only those who need it can have bread.

Here are two more terms for you to learn and add to your collection:

9 **Doubles** are simply pairs of words which almost always go together.
   EXAMPLES: (repetition of the word)   neck and neck   better and better
              (alliterative doubles)   time and tide   bright and breezy
              (opposite doubles)   this and that   up and down
              (repetition of meaning)   rough and tumble   hale and hearty
              (rhyming doubles)   fair and square   high and dry

   For each kind of doubles, think of two more examples.

10 A **Palindrome** is a number, word or phrase that reads the same from right to left as it does from left to right.
   EXAMPLES: (dates)   1991   2002   19.11.91
              (words)   noon   rotator   madam
              (phrases)   nurses run. Able was I ere I saw Elba. (Napoleon)

   a When was the last palindromic date, and when will be the next one?
   b List as many palindromic words as you can think of in ten minutes.

HOMEWORK F3 — HYPERBOLE, LITOTES AND EUPHEMISMS

> YOU NEED TO KNOW ...
> **Hyperbole** (pronounced high-per-bow-lee) is overstatement or exaggeration for effect. It is not intended to deceive anyone and is often used humorously.
> EXAMPLES: *She will kill me if my homework is handed in late.*
> *I've told you that a thousand times since yesterday.*
>
> **Litotes** (pronounced lie-tote-ease) is the opposite of hyperbole. It is understatement, often achieved by using a negative to convey the opposite meaning.
> EXAMPLES: *He's not exactly my best friend.* (meaning: *He is my enemy.*)
> *She is not a bad player.* (meaning: *She is quite a good player.*)

1 Which of these sentences are examples of **hyperbole** and which of **litotes**?

    a She glared at me and I had the feeling that she was not exactly pleased to see me.
    b There were more stars on the stage that night than there were in the sky.
    c He frightened me so much that I must have leapt ten feet into the air.
    d I had not eaten for three days so the food she gave me was not unwelcome.
    e Mount Everest is not the easiest mountain in the world to climb.
    f I'd walk a million miles for one of your smiles.
    g Tarantulas are not the safest creatures to keep as pets.
    h Her blood was boiling and she was so angry that steam was coming out of her ears.

2 For each of these, make up a sentence using **hyperbole** and another using **litotes**.

    a A vicious dog   **b** A quiet town
    c A flooded river   **d** An excited crowd
    e A crowded cafe   **f** A fast car
    g A difficult task   **h** A very large house

> YOU NEED TO KNOW ...
> A **Euphemism** is when a word or phrase is substituted for one which might be thought to be unpleasant, distasteful or embarrassing. For example, instead of saying that someone has *died*, it is frequently said that they have *passed away*; sometimes people refer to the *lavatory* as the *facilities* or any number of other names.

3 These sentences contain euphemisms. Rewrite each one in plain English.

    a It was quite clear that he was a senior citizen.
    b She ran a shop which specialized in dresses for the fuller figure.
    c Not only am I a little off-colour, doctor, but I find I am becoming a little hard of hearing.
    d Uncle Harry is no longer with us, having given up the struggle and departed this life.
    e I think that you are being somewhat economical with the truth.
    f Her clothes had seen better days and it was obvious that she was financially embarrassed.
    g As they approach the evening of their life they are going to live in a retirement hotel.
    h Following a difference of opinion with an officer of the law after taking a drop too much, he found himself a guest of Her Majesty.

Homework F4 — Malapropisms and Spoonerisms

> **You need to know ...**
> A **Malapropism** is the incorrect use of a word. The name comes from a character called Mrs Malaprop in a play by R.B.Sheridan called 'The Rivals'.
> Mrs Malaprop amuses the audience by frequently using the incorrect word.
> Example: she says, "She's as headstrong as an *allegory* on the banks of the Nile" - (*allegory* when she meant *alligator*.)

1. In each sentence write down the words that have been misused, together with the correct words.

   a The infernal compatible engine produces power by burning fools inside the engine itself.
   b Having not eaten all day I am quite ravished and could devolve the providential horse.
   c The practice of having only one husband or one wife is known as monotony.
   d He was under the affluence of alcohol when he hit his head on the lentil over the window.
   e She had a permutation that they would see a ghastly operation in the haunted mention.
   f It said that trespassers would be persecuted but that proved no detergent.
   g Even though he wrote with an inedible pencil it was still ineligible.

2. Make up sentences of your own using **malapropisms** based on these pairs of words that might easily be confused. Where possible, make your sentence amusing.

   a pelvis - pelmet
   b hysterical - historical
   c surgeon - sturgeon
   d septic - sceptic
   e taxi driver - taxidermist
   f corset - corsage
   g banana - bandana
   h personification - perspiration
   i cannonball - cannibal
   j eliminate - illuminate

> **You need to know ...**
> A **spoonerism** was named after a real person - the Rev. W.A.Spooner - who became famous for mixing up the initial sounds of two or more words.
> Example: Spooner said, "A well-boiled icicle" when he meant "A well oiled bicycle".

3. Translate these spoonerisms.

   a You have hissed all my mystery lectures and tasted a whole worm.
   b I once belonged to a scoop of Boy Trouts.
   c Sheets and Kelly are two of my favourite poets.
   d Let us drink a loyal toast to the queer old Dean.
   e Tidy yourself up - crush your boat and hush your brat.
   f 'A Sale of Two Titties' was written by D. Chickens.

4. Try making up some amusing spoonerisms of your own.

HOMEWORK F5   **THREE POETIC DEVICES - LIMERICK, HAIKU, CLERIHEW**

YOU NEED TO KNOW ...
A **Limerick** is a humorous poem of five lines with a rhyming pattern of A-A-B-B-A.
There are usually three stressed beats in the A lines and two stressed beats in the B lines.
Test that out in these
EXAMPLES:

>An epicure dining at Crewe.
>Found quite a large mouse in his stew.
>Said the waiter, "Don't shout.
>And wave it about
>Or the rest will be wanting one too!"   (Anonymous)

>There was an old man of Darjeeling
>Who got on a train bound for Ealing.
>It said on the door,
>"Please don't spit on the floor."
>So he got up and spat on the ceiling.   (Edward Lear)

1   Following the same pattern write two or three limericks of your own.

YOU NEED TO KNOW ...
A **Haiku** is a form of poem which originated in Japan.
It does not need to rhyme but it has a strict pattern of three lines of 5 - 7 - 5 syllables.
The subject matter is frequently to do with nature.
They can be very simple and hauntingly beautiful word pictures.
EXAMPLES:

>The grasshoppers' cry
>Does not reveal how very
>Soon they are to die.   (Basho - 17th Century)

>A flitting firefly!
>"Look! Look there" I start to call;
>But there is no-one.   (Taigi.)

The word itself comes from the Japanese hai - amusement + ku - verse.
The plural of Haiku is haiku not haikus.

2   Write three haiku on: A fallen leaf, A full moon, A stream, (or a subject of your choice.)

YOU NEED TO KNOW ...
A **clerihew** (named after its inventor, Edmund Clerihew Bentley) is a humorous poem of four lines with a rhyming pattern of A-A-B-B. It is about a person whose name forms the first line.

>Sir Christopher Wren
>Said, "I am going to dine with some men.
>If anyone calls
>Say I am designing St Paul's."   (E.C.B.)

>Her Majesty the Queen
>Was too hot to be seen
>In Central Australia
>In all her regalia.   (M.Y.)

3   Write three clerihews about people you know.

SATS PREPARATION - COMPREHENSION PAPERS

'ANNE OF GREEN GABLES'

You are questioned about this passage from 'Anne of Green Gables' in *Homework C1* on Page 27.

This story is set in Canada at the beginning of the Twentieth Century, where Anne Shirley is an orphan. She has recently started at a new school. At that time pupils wrote on framed pieces of slate with chalk crayons.

Gilbert Blythe was trying to make Anne Shirley look at him and failing utterly, because Anne was at that moment totally oblivious, not only of the very existence of Gilbert Blythe, but of every other scholar in Avonlea school and of Avonlea school itself. With her chin propped on her hands and her eyes fixed on the blue glimpse of the Lake of Shining Waters that the west window afforded, she was far away in a gorgeous dreamland, hearing and seeing nothing save her own wonderful visions.

Gilbert Blythe wasn't used to putting himself out to make a girl look at him and meeting with failure. She should look at him, that red-haired Shirley girl with the little pointed chin and the big eyes that weren't like the eyes of any other girl in Avonlea school.

Gilbert reached across the aisle, picked up the end of Anne's long braid, held it out at arm's length and said in a piercing whisper: "Carrots! Carrots!"

Then Anne looked at him with a vengeance! She did more than look. She sprang to her feet, her bright fancies fallen into careless ruin. She flashed one indignant glance at Gilbert from eyes whose angry sparkle was swiftly quenched in equally angry tears.

"You mean, hateful boy!" she exclaimed passionately. "How dare you!"

And then - Thwack! Anne had brought her slate down on Gilbert's head and cracked it - slate, not head - clear across.

Avonlea school always enjoyed a scene. This was an especially enjoyable one. Everybody said, "Oh!" in horrified delight. Diana gasped. Ruby Gillis, who was inclined to be hysterical, began to cry. Tommy Sloane let his team of crickets escape him altogether while he stared open-mouthed at the tableau.

Mr Phillips stalked down the aisle and laid his hand heavily on Anne's shoulder.

"Anne Shirley, what does this mean?" he said angrily.

Anne returned no answer. It was asking too much of flesh and blood to expect her to tell before the whole school that she had been called "carrots." Gilbert it was who spoke up stoutly. "It was my fault, Mr Phillips. I teased her."

Mr Phillips paid no heed to Gilbert.

"I am sorry to see a pupil of mine displaying such a temper and such a vindictive spirit," he said in a solemn tone, as if the mere fact of being a pupil of his ought to root out all evil passions from the hearts of small imperfect mortals. "Anne, go and stand on the platform in front of the blackboard for the rest of the afternoon."

Anne would have infinitely preferred a whipping to this punishment, under which her sensitive spirit quivered as from a whiplash. With a white, set face she obeyed. Mr Phillips took a chalk crayon and wrote on the blackboard above her head:

"Ann Shirley has a very bad temper. Ann Shirley must learn to control her temper," and then read it out loud so that even the primer class, who couldn't read writing, should understand it.

Anne stood there for the rest of the afternoon with that legend above her. She did not cry or hang her head. Anger was still too hot in her heart for that and it sustained her amid all her agony of humiliation. With resentful eyes and passion-red cheeks she confronted alike Diana's sympathetic gaze and Charlie Sloane's indignant nods and Josie Pye's malicious smiles. As for Gilbert Blythe, she would not even look at him. She would never look at him again! She would never speak to him!!

When school was dismissed Anne marched out with her red head held high. Gilbert Blythe tried to intercept her at the porch door.

"I'm awfully sorry I made fun of your hair, Anne," he whispered contritely. "Honest I am. Don't be mad at me for keeps, now."

Anne swept by disdainfully without look or sign of hearing. "Oh, how could you, Anne?" breathed Diana as they went down the road, half reproachfully, half admiringly. Diana felt that she could never have resisted Gilbert's plea.

"I shall never forgive Gilbert Blythe," said Anne firmly. "And Mr Phillips spelled my name without an e too. The iron has entered into my soul, Diana."

Diana hadn't the least idea what Anne meant, but she understood that it was something terrible.

from 'Anne of Green Gables' by L. M. Montgomery.

HOMEWORK C1 (40 MINUTES)

Spend about ten minutes reading carefully the passage from 'Anne of Green Gables' on Pages 25 and 26. You must become used to working within strict time limits. Then spend about ten minutes working on Question 1 and about twenty minutes on Question 2.

Refer to words and phrases in the passage to support your ideas.

1 What impression do you get of Anne Shirley's nature?

In your answer you should comment on:

- her thoughts before and after the incident;
- how she reacts to the other characters in the story.

2 How does the writer, L. M. Montgomery, make you feel increasingly sorry for Anne?

In your answer you should comment on:

- the way Anne is described;
- the way she reacts to Gilbert's remarks about the colour of her hair;
- the way in which the teacher, Mr Philips, treats Anne;
- the way other members of the class respond to the incident.

HOMEWORK C2 (25 MINUTES)

Spend about five minutes reading the information about Brookstone School on Page 28. Take no more than 20 minutes to answer this question.

In what ways does this fact-sheet try to persuade the reader of the merits of Brookstone School?

In your answer you should comment on:

- how much is directed towards prospective parents and how much towards their children;
- how the writer may have selected information in order to persuade the reader;
- the way words and layout are used to create a positive image of the school;
- how much this fact-sheet would make you wish to attend Brookstone if you happened to be in the position of someone looking for a new school.

Welcome to
BROOKSTONE SCHOOL

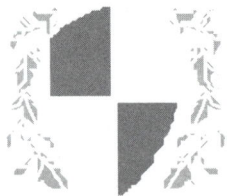

Brookstone School

Thank you for your interest in Brookstone School. This Information Sheet can but give you a mere flavour of this unique and caring educational establishment. Please come and visit us if you would like to know more, and talk to our students, who are the focus of everything we do here. They will be pleased to show you around and answer any questions you may have. For an appointment please telephone 01328 927364

EXAMINATION RESULTS

Brookstone's overall GCSE results continue to score well above the national average. While examination success is not considered to be of paramount importance in the philosophy of this forward-thinking school, we are nevertheless proud of the fact that in last year's entry students achieved an average of 6.3 A to C passes while 14 boys and 6 girls gained 9 or more passes.

DISCIPLINE

We are frequently asked by prospective parents about discipline. It would be foolish to say that we do not have disciplinary problems at Brookstone but those few that do occur are dealt with by the School Council which is made up of an elected group of students from all year groups, staff and parents. Students at Brookstone are given responsibility for their own school at an early age and we find that they value it.

UNIFORM

Brookstone maintains the highest traditions of School Uniform. Two years ago consultation with students, parents, staff and governors resulted in an overwhelming demand to retain uniform and led to the design of the present, highly practical dress code. The distinctive school colours of red and black prevail in the fashionable designs of 'smart casual' for both boys and girls, with enough choice of style to please even the most individual students. Year 11 Design and Technology students are responsible for the annual review of Uniform design.

CURRICULUM

In addition to fulfilling all the requirements of the National Curriculum, Brookstone is proud of its many achievements in other fields. In the Arts, innovative courses in Art, Music and Drama have led to extension work including Media Studies which is attracting national recognition. Our School of Language is the constant recipient of praise. Nine languages are currently taught at Brookstone and last year 97 of our students spent some time studying abroad in France, Germany, Russia and Japan.

THE BROOKSTONE SPORTS FOUNDATION was set up eighteen years ago by a group of successful old Brookstonians. Since that time it has provided a range of Sports facilities second to none. We are pleased to announce that with funding from the National Lottery work will start this year on the building of a new complex which will incorporate a swimming pool, gymnasia and indoor running track. We look forward to seeing even more Brookstone students performing at national events in the future.

The three homeworks on this page are designed to test your writing.
Spend about 40 minutes on each task.

You will be assessed on:

- your ideas and the way you organise and express them;
- your ability to write clearly, using paragraphs and accurate punctuation, spelling and grammar.

HOMEWORK C3

Imagine that you have been invited to talk to a meeting of new pupils about your school.

Write your speech, in which you try to make the new pupils feel welcome and quell any anxieties they might have, while at the same time trying to give an honest picture of your school.

You may include any aspects of school life you wish.

HOMEWORK C4

Write about an incident of injustice at school.

You could:

- write about a real or imaginary event;
- try to create a feeling of sympathy for your central character.

HOMEWORK C5

Write a letter to your Headteacher in which you outline changes which you feel may need to be made in order to make your school more appropriate to the Twenty-first Century.

You could:

- consider matters of curriculum, discipline, buildings and equipment;
- consider how you believe your ideas might make the school more attractive to prospective parents and their children.

"Hopi's Story"

Hopi is a young Amazonian Indian living in the great rainforest. In his short life he has seen his tribe broken up as a result of the systematic destruction of their environment. In the past year his parents and grandfather have all died. The uncles have gone north leaving Hopi living alone with his wife and son.

Hopi lay in the darkness of the hut, wondering what had woken him. He listened to the gentle, regular breathing of his wife beside him on the sleeping platform and reached out to feel the warm little body of their infant son who stirred for a moment before snuggling into his mother once more. Hopi rose and crept silently out of the hut into the night, The chill dampness of the air on his naked body told him that dawn must be close while all around him the muted sounds of the living jungle told him of no intruder. But something had disturbed his sleep.

Swiftly Hopi climbed the great tree beneath which they had built their hut. Through the upper canopy of leaves he was able to see the last faint stars fading in the first shadow of the dawn. Soon the jungle would be an almost deafening cacophony of noise as the thousands of different birds squawked and whistled and cried out, claiming their territories. With closed eyes he lay against the slender upper branches, swaying almost imperceptibly in the the movement of the air.

Hopi's eyes opened in sudden fear and his nostrils flared. Smoke! That must have been what had awoken him. On the air he detected the faint but unmistakable smell of burning trees. Higher still he climbed until from the topmost branch of the great tree he was able to look out over the dense vista of green, stretching in all directions as far as the eye could see. As the light gathered strength swirling clouds of mist crept around the root of the jungle but Hopi's eyes strained to see a different kind of cloud. Hopi had been just a boy when the white farmers first came to tear down and burn the trees. Many of the villagers were tempted by the bright toys and trappings of these new men and had gone to work for them. Hopi's grandfather had shaken his head, saying that no good would come of it, that it was against the laws of the rainforest. Many had laughed at the old man but he had been right. The food the white men gave them made them ill and soon there were diseases which killed. Finally a great fire had burned in the wind and destroyed their village but Hopi's family had escaped with their lives, moving deeper into the jungle. From there they observed the white men bringing in countless herds of strange beasts to devour the lush grass which sprang up on the cleared land; but each year they wanted more and each year Hopi saw the life-giving forest being turned into a desert wasteland.

Now his worst fears were confirmed. Not more than a day's walk away he saw the smoke rising in the early light of the day and he knew that the army of men and machines was on the move once again.

Leaping skilfully down from branch to branch Hopi was quickly on the ground. Ata stood waiting for him, heavy with the child that would soon be born, their little son straddling her tiny hips and gurgling happily. Instantly she sensed that something was amiss and recognising the despair in her husband's eyes she knew that once again they would be forced to move away, to find a new place to live. This was not a good time.

"When?" she asked. There was never the need for many words between them.

Hopi could not bear to see the fear in his wife's big brown eyes and he looked away.

"Soon!" he replied.

It was sooner than they thought. Two weeks after the time Hopi had first smelled the smoke, the baby still had not come. Ata knew that it should have been born but something was wrong and she was so tired. Hopi knew that he must fetch help but the nearest village was a day's walk, perhaps more, to the north. He left enough food and water for three days and set off in the early dawn before Ata awoke. She would see the provisions and know that he had gone.

Hopi did not spare himself and by nightfall he had arrived at the village. No-one was willing to go back with him, no matter how he pleaded, but an ancient crone who reminded him of his grandmother took him to one side. The forest was the great provider, full of plants which could cure all kinds of ailments. The old woman gave him a bundle of dried leaves and berries with elaborate instructions about how he should administer them so that he set out for the return journey the following day more hopefully.

It was mid-morning when Hopi became aware of a change. Looking up through the giant trees he was aware of the gathering movement of a rising wind in the leaves of the upper branches. With fires not far away he knew what dangers winds could bring and with growing anxiety he began to run, careless of the lower vegetation which whipped and scratched and tore at him as he passed.

In the warm darkness of the hut Ata drifted in and out of consciousness. The pain was great and she had lost all track of the days. The baby crawled around, hungry and fractious but she did not have the strength to do anything about him. There was the smell of smoke, much stronger now, and outside she could hear the sound of the whole forest on the move it seemed, animals and birds, creatures of every description squealing and squawking as they fled in panic before the approaching fire.

Finally Hopi came to the rim of the last valley separating him from his wife and son. The sight which met his eyes made him cry aloud. Through the bottom of the valley the fire was spreading like a river, the flames leaping from treetop to treetop, sending a lurid red and orange glow into the gathering dusk. Perhaps more terrifying was the noise, even at this distance, a great roaring and crackling, punctuated by deafening splitting sounds as huge trees, many hundreds of years old, seemed to explode, sending fountains of sparks high into the sky. Hopi threw back his head and howled like a stricken animal as he realised that the fire was completely blocking his way back.

HOMEWORK C6 (40 MINUTES)

Spend about ten minutes reading carefully the passage about the Amazonian Indians on Pages 30 and 31.
Spend about ten minutes working on Question 1 and about 20 minutes on Question 2.

Refer to words and phrases in the passage to support your ideas.

1   What does the passage tell you about the relationship between Hopi and his wife?

In your answer you should comment on:

- Hopi's thoughts and fears about how the destruction of their environment will affect their lives;
- how they have little need for language.

2   In what ways does the writer convey the hopelessness of Hopi and Ata's situation?

In your answer you should comment on:

- why Hopi, Ata and their son are alone at this point in the story;
- the reasons for Hopi's desperate journey to the village;
- Ata's feelings as she waits in the smoky hut;
- Hopi's reaction when he sees the fire in the valley.

HOMEWORK C7 (25 MINUTES)

Spend about five minutes reading the information about the Destruction of Planet Earth on Page 33.
Take no more than 20 minutes to answer this question.

In what ways does this fact-sheet set out to increase the reader's awareness of pollution on an international scale?

In your answer you should comment on

- the overall concentration of alarming 'facts';
- how the writer may have selected information in order to shock the reader;
- how successful you feel the sheet might be in stirring its readers into action;
- the extent to which you think that what is written is in fact indisputable, especially in the paragraph entitled "Atmospheric Pollution".

The Destruction of Planet Earth

Atmospheric Pollution - Every day we pump countless tonnes of pollutants into our atmosphere, into the air we breathe. There are many sources of air pollution but the main ones are factories and vehicle emissions. The results - acid rain, the depletion of the ozone layer and global warming - are a serious threat to the future of our planet.

Acid Rain is created by a cocktail of chemicals being carried around the world in rain clouds and falling as sulphuric and nitric acid. It is estimated that in some parts of the world as many as three out of every five trees are damaged by acid rain and in places whole forests have been destroyed. Where it falls into lakes it is capable of killing almost all of the fish that live there.

The Ozone Layer surrounds the Earth and protects us from harmful ultraviolet radiation from the sun. Chemicals such as CFCs (chlorofluorocarbons) have caused a hole the size of the United States in the ozone layer. CFCs, like carbon dioxide, are also greenhouse gases, which gather in the upper atmosphere and lead to global warming.

Rainforests have been described as the lungs of the World. They absorb carbon dioxide from the air and release oxygen. Without them we could not live and yet we are destroying them at an alarming rate. As well as being the home of some 200 million tribal people they are a treasury of animals, birds, insects and plants. Once a species becomes extinct it can never be replaced and yet we are destroying species at an unbelievable rate of 50 per day. An area of forest the size of England, Scotland and Wales is destroyed every year to make way for unsuitable short-term projects such as cattle farming. Once the trees have gone the land soon loses its nutrients and becomes useless for grazing and the farmers move on to destroy yet more forest. What a terrible waste!

The North Sea - Of all the oceans of the world, our own North Sea is among the most polluted. Raw sewage, heavy metals, organic chemicals and nuclear wastes are all dumped into the sea, causing untold problems to the creatures which live there. Many fish are found to be suffering from tumours, bacterial ulcers and liver damage. Grey seals, which live on these fish, are being discovered with liver cancers and the breakdown of their immune systems, a disease similar to AIDS in humans. Do you eat fish?

Asthma - In the past ten years the number of children suffering from asthma has increased by 400 per cent. Doctors blame poor air quality.

These indisputable facts are part of a growing international problem, and not enough is being done to halt the systematic destruction of our planet.

For more information, write to:
- Department of the Environment, 43, Marsham St., London SW1P 3PY
- Nature Conservancy Council, Northminster House, Peterborough, Cambs. PE1 1UA
- Young People's Trust for the Environment and Nature Conservation, 95, Woodbridge Rd., Guildford, Surrey GU1 4PY

The three homeworks on this page are designed to test your writing.
Spend about 40 minutes on each task.

You will be assessed on:

- your ideas and the way you organise and express them;
- your ability to write clearly, using paragraphs and accurate punctuation, spelling and grammar.

HOMEWORK C8

Imagine that you have been invited to speak about pollution in your school assembly.

Write your speech, in which you try to make fellow pupils aware of the enormous dangers of pollution as well as offering suggestions about ways in which they, as individuals, might do something to help.

You may include any aspects of pollution you wish.

HOMEWORK C9

Write a story set in a future where nothing has been done to halt international pollution.

You could:

- write in the first person, as a kind of diary entry, or in the third person;
- comment on how different aspects of pollution have affected the quality of life for your central character.

HOMEWORK C10

Write a letter to a world leader of your choice in which you appeal to them to do something positive to prevent further pollution of our planet.

You could:

- make detailed suggestions about one or two aspects of pollution;
- appeal to their position of power and what they owe to future generations.

From "The Myrtle and the Ivy"

The year is 1916. Charlotte is a young woman of 22 who has volunteered to serve as a nurse in the Great War. Because she is able to drive, she finds herself posted to France, to the Western Front, as an ambulance driver. At this point in the story she has no idea that her brother, George, has come from India and is just a few miles down the line.

Charlotte never forgot her first sight of the field hospital. She had thought of herself by now as a trained nurse, pretty well inured to most forms of human suffering, but the sheer volume of patients and the severity of their wounds affected her deeply. On the whole it was their extreme youth that shocked her for here were the brave lads who had marched away with such noble thoughts and hopes, all thinking that it was going to be a great and glorious adventure. Those who had lost arms or legs or sight did not think that now.

It was heartbreaking work and it was several weeks before Charlotte could deal with her patients with any degree of detachment; but shut out her feelings she must, or go mad. Conditions for the nurses were not ideal either and it was only the presence of her friend Kate who made it bearable for they were huddled into dark, evil-smelling huts with rudimentary sanitation and crammed into bunk beds that were so hard that only their acute exhaustion allowed them to sleep. It worried Charlotte, as a nurse, that she never felt entirely clean but there was nothing they could do about it and by the end of three months she felt as though she had been there for years. Her whole concentration was bent on keeping warm and as clean as possible.

Sometimes, when there had been a battle, they were on duty for days at a stretch and the wounded came from all over the fronts; at other times they were left to deal with the men who were suffering as a result of the appalling conditions under which they were obliged to live - if one could call it living.

There was an ailment known as trench foot, when constant standing in mud and puddles of water contrived to rot the men's feet; there was extreme malnutrition and illnesses like pneumonia; but also there was the sheer terror which many of them suffered from as a result of being in a war situation.

This was often the hardest to help as men retreated into worlds of their own and started at the least sound. Loss of limbs they could understand but the mind was a different thing and not all recruits received the sympathetic handling that they should have. Most of the cases were sent home to England, to a country that found it hard to realise that young men could return so shattered.

But there were times when there were no battles and nothing seemed to happen for days on end as they waited, and waited. Then boredom would set in but there were always snipers ready to take a pot shot so that there could be no let-up in the armies' vigilance and it became a war of nerves. To keep the men occupied more and more trenches were built in the thick mud. Men stood for hours in the pouring rain, their only companions the multitudes of rats with which they shared their trenches.

* * * * * * * * * *

George constantly marvelled at the stoicism of his comrades, especially as they were on very short rations and as well as the constant rain the weather was now becoming very cold. He smiled wryly to himself, remembering how he had dared to complain about the heat in India. He could wish for some of it now! When they were not in the thick of fighting he wrote letters home and read and re-read the few books he had brought with him. Sadly they were almost falling to bits in the damp but they did manage to take his mind off the conditions for a few hours as he lay in his bunk, wrapped in his greatcoat and boots and an army blanket, trying not to think of baths and lashings of hot water and all the comforts of life before the War.

He drew his writing wallet before him and sitting on an upturned box tried to commence a letter to his mother. Before the war he had always enjoyed the pleasure of putting pen to paper and he had a vivid command of language that always made his reader feel that he was there. Now it was so difficult.

How could he tell his mother of the unspeakable horrors he had witnessed since coming to France and of the terrible privations that they were forced to endure? He had seen men who had shared breakfast with him drop at his feet, killed by a sniper's bullet; he had been forced to watch them die a long lingering death because no one dared venture into the part known as No Man's Land; or he had seen grown men weep through fear, knowing that it was he who had to force them to leave the discomfort of the trenches to face the horrors that awaited them outside. They were ill equipped and the rations were monotonous, tins of bully beef and hard biscuits that had to be dunked into billy cans to soften them.

Parcels from home were not as plentiful as those in Britain imagined. It was difficult for a package actually to reach the person for whom it was and more often than not the soldier could be dead before it arrived. George was uncertain how much those left at home knew of the war. Sometimes a returning soldier brought back a tattered copy of the Times which spoke of 'our brave boys at the front' and how near victory they were and how they were all heroes. Where was Charlotte he wondered? At least he knew she would understand something of the realities of war because the last he had heard of her was that she was nursing the wounded in Bristol. Many of the men at times secretly hoped for a "Blighty" as they were known, that was a wound that meant they could be sent home and not have to return to the Front.

Now there was the added danger of gas - stifling-hot mustard gas that reached the lungs and choked a man to death. They had all been issued with gas masks but they were cumbersome to carry and in the first wave the men did not bother with them. Now they accepted them as part of the burden they must shoulder. Wearily George searched through the wallet and brought out one of the post cards they were issued with and ticked the line that simply said, "I am well. Letter to follow soon."

| HOMEWORK C11 | (40 MINUTES) |

Remember to divide your time sensibly. Spend no more than ten minutes studying the passage on the previous two pages from a novel about the First World War.
You may make brief notes if you wish but it is perhaps more important simply to enjoy the passage and gain an overall impression of the two points of view – Charlotte's and George's.

Ten minutes working on Question 1 should be adequate, leaving twenty minutes to deal with Question 2 which will carry more marks.

Refer to words and phrases in the passage to support your ideas.

1 How does George's view of the war differ from that of Charlotte's?

   In your answer you should comment on:

   - Charlotte's priorities, her feelings and her concerns;
   - George's feelings and responsibilities towards his family and the men under his command.

2 How successfully do you feel that the writer has managed to portray the different views of a woman and a man?

   In your answer you should comment on:

   - the immediacy of Charlotte's viewpoint;
   - how George considers matters from a wider, military point of view;
   - how the writer has selected information;
   - the words the writer has selected to create a vivid picture of life at the Front.

| HOMEWORK C12 | (25 MINUTES) |

Spend five minutes reading the two poems on the next page.
Notice that the two poets portray quite different images of war - one showing the glory and the honour, while the other tries to show the reader something of the horror of war.
Take no more than 20 minutes to answer this question.

How does each poet try to achieve the intended effect on his reader?

In your answer you should comment on:

- the images each has chosen to include;
- the kinds of words and expressions each has used;
- which poet has been most successful from your point of view.

Two Poems About War

The Soldier by Rupert Brooke

If I should die, think only this of me;
    That there's some corner of a foreign field
That is for ever England. There shall be
    In that rich earth a richer dust concealed;
A dust whom England bore, shaped, made aware,
    Gave, once, her flowers to love, her ways to roam,
A body of England's, breathing English air,
    Washed by the rivers, blest by suns of home.

And think, this heart, all evil shed away,
    A pulse in the eternal mind, no less
    Gives somewhere back the thoughts by England given;
Her sights and sounds; dreams happy as her day;
    And laughter, learnt of friends; and gentleness,
    In hearts at peace, under an English heaven.

Anthem for Doomed Youth by Wilfred Owen

What passing bells for those who die as cattle?
    Only the monstrous anger of the guns.
    Only the stuttering rifles' rapid rattle
Can patter out their hasty orisons.
No mockeries now for them; no prayers nor bells,
    Nor any voice of mourning save the choirs, -
The shrill, demented choirs of wailing shells;
    And bugles calling them from sad shires.

What candles may be held to speed them all?
    Not in the hands of boys, but in their eyes
Shall shine the holy glimmers of goodbyes.
    The pallor of girls' brows shall be their pall;
Their flowers the tenderness of patient minds,
    And each slow dusk a drawing-down of blinds.

The three homeworks on this page are designed to test your writing.
Spend about 40 minutes on each task. You will be assessed on:

- your ideas and the way you organise and express them;
- your ability to write clearly, using paragraphs and accurate punctuation, spelling and grammar.

HOMEWORK C13

Imagine that you are a television reporter who has been sent to a modern day war zone.

Write your report ready for transmission on the evening's main news bulletin.

You may include any aspects of war you think you may be likely to encounter.

HOMEWORK C14

Write an entry in a diary which shows that war is not so much about armies and one country fighting another, but about the effects which it has on individuals, ordinary men and women, and their families.

HOMEWORK C15

In the extract from "The Myrtle and the Ivy" George found himself unable to write to his mother. Write a letter from George to his brother in which he is brutally honest.

You should:

- write about the terrible conditions in which they are forced to live;
- include his feelings about the terrible waste and futility of war.

"Shirley Vane"

Shirley Vane is a woman in her early forties who has spent her life caring for her invalid mother. The mother has died recently and at this point in the story Shirley has set out on a long-dreamed-of holiday to Spain.

"There isn't a view of the sea," she began nervously. "I thought I'd be able to see the sea."

The young woman at the representatives' desk looked up and automatically flashed a plastic smile at the middle-aged and slightly faded woman in the navy blue cardigan. Her eyes travelled downwards, taking in the long, pleated skirt, the sandals and tights. In this heat! She had noticed her on the coach from the airport, sitting alone, anxiously clutching a large handbag. Having worked for the travel company for seven years, Sharon had seen it all before. They came in all shapes and sizes and she had become cynical in the way she could now pigeon-hole a plane-load of holiday-makers on sight.

This one fell into her least favourite category: "single, first-time traveller, not much money, potential complainer".

"What name?" she enquired, brightly, extracting a list from the pile of paper before her.

"Vane. Shirley Vane."

"Ah, yes, here we are, Miss Vane. Room 493. That's in the North Wing. Beautiful view of the mountains," she enthused. "Everything all right in the room, is it?"

"Well, I suppose, but ..."

"I know, you were hoping for a sea view. Unfortunately the rooms at the front with the balconies are all doubles or family rooms. Well, I say 'unfortunately' but between you and me those rooms get the full sun and they get very hot. You're really much better off where you are," the professional rep. continued, the smile still in place.

"Ah, I see," Shirley said uncertainly, not at all sure that she did see.

"Anyway, hopefully you won't be spending much time in your room. There's so much to do. See you at the welcome meeting at two o'clock, I hope." With that she gathered her papers together dismissively.

Shirley took a deep breath and made a final attempt. "Er ... I'm not one to complain, but the room is very small."

The smile faded. "Now look, Miss Vane, it is a single room. That's what you paid for and that's what a single room is like. I don't know what you were expecting. I really don't."

Shirley Vane was easily intimidated. "Yes. Yes, of course. I'm sorry."

Sharon believed in letting them know from the start who was in charge. Pleased with her success, she treated the woman to another smile. "That's quite all right. It's what we're here for. See you at two." As Shirley turned to go, she added, "And Miss Vane, if you don't mind me saying, you'll be much too hot in those tights."

Shirley blushed and scuttled away, holding her cardigan around her defensively.

To while away the time until the meeting, Shirley wandered around the huge complex of the hotel. It was clear that when it had been built in the first heady days of package holidays it must have been luxurious but now the splendour had faded into a shabbiness which Shirley found both exotic and comfortable. The main reception area was high-ceilinged, the black marble floor making it remarkably cool. At this time of day it was quiet apart from two maids mopping the floor in a desultory fashion and chatting in a language Shirley did not recognise. There was an unhurried peace in the way they approached their task which she found quite soothing.

Going outside the white light of midday reflected off the pool, almost blinding, and the heat enveloped her like a heavy blanket. All the white plastic loungers were either occupied by glistening, scantily clad bodies or there were towels conspicuously claiming ownership, although only a few people were actually in the water. Making her way around the poolside to the bar area where she thought the meeting was to take place, Shirley felt horribly over-dressed and she moved stiffly, awkwardly aware of the curious stares the week-long-established sunbathers reserved for the newcomers.

As she approached the little thatched bar one of the waiters said something to his friend who looked directly at Shirley and laughed. She knew he was laughing at her and she felt her cheeks burning in indignation.

Head held high, she asked, "Excuse me. Is this where the meeting is to take place?"
The one who had laughed still mocked her with his eyes, replying in a heavy accent, "Meeting? What meeting? Is no meeting now."

"Two o'clock," Shirley explained patiently. "There is a welcome meeting with Torrinos Travel at two o'clock. It said it was at the poolside bar."

"Poolside bar. Si. Is here," he said, waving his arms and grinning to his friend.
"But it's almost two now and there's no-one here," she insisted.

The waiter laughed loudly and Shirley was aware of several of the nearby sunbathers listening to the exchange. "No, lady," he laughed, "is not two o'clock."

"But I assure you it is. It said on the notice that the meeting was at two o'clock." She spoke slowly and clearly, trying to make him understand.

"No, no, no lady. Meeting is two o'clock. But now, time is only twelve o'clock," he explained equally slowly, but carefully as though speaking to a child. "You forget to change watch, si?"

Again Shirley felt her cheeks flaming with embarrassment. How could she make such a stupid mistake?

The first waiter took pity on her. "Not to worry lady. You have drink of limon. On the house, si?" he said, shovelling ice into a tall glass.

Shirley Vane kept her eyes lowered so that they should not see the hurt and the fear in them.

HOMEWORK C16 (40 MINUTES)

Spend about 10 minutes reading carefully the passage on the previous pages.
Spend about 10 minutes working on Question 1 and about 20 minutes on Question 2.

Refer to words and phrases in the passage to support your ideas.

1. Do you think that this was the wrong kind of holiday for Shirley Vane?

   In your answer you should comment on:

   - her first impressions of the hotel;
   - how she reacts to the other characters in the story.

2. How does the writer create sympathy for Shirley?

   In your answer you should comment on:

   - the way she is described;
   - the way she allows Sharon to defeat her so easily;
   - the way the Spanish waiters treat her and her reactions.

HOMEWORK C17 (25 MINUTES - 5 MINUTES READING, 20 MINUTES WRITING.)

How useful do you consider the following Holiday Information to be?

In your answer you should comment on:

- how much is aimed at promoting the company and how much is genuinely useful information;
- how the writer may have selected information in order to persuade the reader;
- the way words and layout are used to create a positive image of the company;
- how much is included just to safeguard the company against possible complaints from holidaymakers.

SYDONI TRAVEL

ESSENTIAL HOLIDAY INFORMATION
Thank you for choosing to book your holiday with Sydoni Travel. Our primary aim is your satisfaction. Please take the time to read the information on this page and contact our Helpline with any queries you have.

ACCOMMODATION
Standards in foreign hotels vary widely. At Sydoni Travel we inspect all hotels before including them in our brochure and we hope that our Star ratings are a useful guide, varying from a One-Star award for basic facilities to the extreme luxury of the Five-Star award.

REPRESENTATIVES
All Sydoni representatives are highly trained. Their first duty is to ensure that your holiday goes smoothly. If you have any cause for complaint, please contact your representative immediately - do not leave it until it is too late to do anything. In your hotel you will find the times when he or she is on duty, but in emergency you will be able to make contact 24 hours a day. Your Sydoni representative will be happy to advise you about local activities and excursions and can arrange car hire for you.

A FEW FLYING FACTS
Sydoni Travel uses only scheduled flights on national airlines and therefore the conditions of the carrier apply to all passengers. Where delays occur it must be recognised that these are out of the control of Sydoni. Seats may be reserved at the time of booking, subject to availability. Children aged two and above must have their own seats on the aircraft. We remind passengers that it is dangerous to fly less than 48 hours after scuba diving.

EXCURSIONS
On arrival at your resort your representative will offer you a varied selection of excursions, carefully planned to show you the best a particular country has to offer. You may be offered similar trips locally at lower prices but please remember that all Sydoni excursions include the services of a trained, English-speaking Sydoni guide and full insurance. Beware of imitations!

WHAT'S INCLUDED
- Return flights from UK to resort.
- Transfers to and from resort.
- All airport taxes.
- Accommodation as shown on your invoice.
- Continental breakfast.
- Hotel service charges.
- The services of a Sydoni representative.
- VAT on all holidays within the EU.

WHAT'S NOT INCLUDED
- Holiday Insurance (obligatory).
- Flight supplements. (see p 104)
- Optional excursions.
- Cost of inoculations.
- Some hotel facilities such as sunbeds, air conditioning, safety deposit boxes, saunas, sports and equipment.
- Extra facilities such as laundry, room service, drinks.

THE SYDONI PROMISE
Sydoni is renowned for giving its holidaymakers a fair deal. If we change the date of your holiday, the named accommodation or your departure airport we will reduce the holiday price by up to 50%, depending on the length of notice we are able to give.

These three homeworks are designed to test your writing.

Spend about 40 minutes on each task. You will be assessed on:

- your ideas and the way you organise and express them;
- your ability to write clearly, use paragraphs, punctuation, spelling and grammar.

HOMEWORK C18

Imagine that you are a holiday rep. welcoming new holidaymakers to a resort.

Write your speech, in which you try to make all the holidaymakers feel welcome, but at the same time you have to try to sell them as many excursions as possible because much of your pay is commission on these sales.

You may base this on a resort in this country or abroad.

HOMEWORK C19

Write about a holiday which went dreadfully wrong.

You could:

- write about a real or imaginary event;
- try to create a feeling of sympathy for your central character.

HOMEWORK C20

Write a letter to a Holiday Travel Company in which you complain about a holiday which did not live up to the promises of their brochure.

You could:

- relate this to matters of accommodation, food, treatment by their rep. or any other aspect of a holiday.
- how you believe the company should produce a brochure which is far more honest than the ones we usually see?

A Wet Tuesday

In this story Colin and his parents are on holiday and visit an Animal Rescue Centre.

A lady in the very modern Reception area greeted them and told them that they were most welcome to look around. "Anything you want to know, just ask any of the staff."

First they went to the Small Animal Building and looked at a room with cages containing rabbits of every shape, size and colour. Next door were mice, gerbils and rats which made Sue shudder so she was glad to move on to the next building which housed the cats. The conditions in which the cats were kept was really impressive, with each one in its own little glass-fronted room with a cosy cat-bed. A flap led to an outside area and it was all spotlessly clean. David said he thought it was a five-star hotel for cats. Most appeared to be contented, curled up in their beds, or sitting, watching their visitors with big green eyes. One big, old, grey cat was clearly less happy and arched its back and spat when they looked in at him. There were several litters of small kittens with high-pitched, pitiful cries but there were notices on all the cages indicating that they were all booked to go to homes.

As they moved into the Kennels area all the dogs started barking and running up and down in their cages. The noise was deafening. A huge German Shepherd threw itself in the air in a series of wild somersaults. Two heavy black dogs stood side by side and barked, a deep, hollow sound. Next to them a funny little dog with a beard ran in circles, chasing its tail and yapping.

In the far corner of the end cage lay a miserable bundle of grey fur. It slowly lifted its head and Colin found himself looking into the saddest pair of eyes he had ever seen. The animal stared at him for a long moment before its head sank back down.

'That's Wolf", the kennel maid, who was called Janice, said. "Poor old thing! When we found him he had several broken ribs and from what we could tell his owner had held him by the tail and kicked him almost to death. He also had several cigarette burns. He's mended physically but you don't know what scars they carry inside."

Sue was listening. "How can people be so cruel to a poor, dumb animal?" she asked.

"Oh you'd be surprised," Janice replied. "Some of what I've seen here would make you weep. Poor Wolf, he's been with us for six months and nobody wants him. He hates being caged."

"What will happen to him?" Mike asked.

The kennel maid hesitated, looking at Colin and wondering how much to say. "Of course we do our best to find homes for all our dogs but … well sometimes it just isn't possible and we simply haven't the room to keep dogs for ever."

"Meaning you'll have him put to sleep," Colin stated bluntly. Sue could see he was upset.

"Sometimes it's the best thing to do," Janice tried to explain. "He's a desperately unhappy dog, as you can see. He doesn't eat properly and sometimes in the night he howls."

"Is that why you called him 'Wolf'?" Colin asked.

"Not really," Janice explained. "It's his breed - he's an Irish Wolfhound."

Colin was standing next to his father. He placed his two hands, thumb to thumb, finger tip to finger tip, around his father's wrist. It was a habit he had. "Dad …"

"No! Don't even think it," Mike said in a tone that invited no argument. "Anyway, look at the time. If we're going to find somewhere to eat, we'd better make a move," and with that he strode purposefully off towards the car.

"Mum …" Colin began.

"Colin, you know how your father feels. After Hamlet died we were all so upset he swore we'd never have another dog." Turning to Janice, Sue explained, "Hamlet was a wonderful dog - he was a Great Dane. He died nearly a year ago now and we still miss him terribly."

Two weeks later the Carter family car was once again winding its way down the leafy, country lanes. Today it was not raining; instead, the sun chased the shadows of clouds across the green hills. Mike was strangely silent and tight-lipped. Beside him Sue turned slowly to look over her shoulder. In the back seat Colin sat very still and upright, eyes wide and scarcely daring to breathe, while beside him, equally upright and with an expression almost of disbelief on his hairy face, sat none other than the wolfhound.

Mike pulled into a lay-by and stopped. Turning around he looked at the boy and the dog, and the stern look on his face melted into a smile. "Well?" he said.

Colin was almost choked with the emotion of it all. "Thanks, Dad," he mumbled. "Thanks, Mum. Thanks a million."

Mike reached over the back and went to stroke the dog, but he cowered away, as though afraid that he was going to receive a blow, and he leaned towards Colin who put a protective arm around his bony shoulder.

"That dog's going to need a great deal of love and care," said Sue. "You're going to have quite a task ahead of you, Colin."

| HOMEWORK C21 | (40 MINUTES) |

The story on Pages 45 and 46 describes the Carter family's visit to an Animal Rescue Centre and how their son, Colin, takes pity on one of the dogs in the cages.

Spend about ten minutes reading the passage carefully, ten minutes working on Question 1 and about twenty minutes on Question 2.

Support your ideas by referring to words and phrases in the passage.

1   What impression do you get of the Animal Rescue Centre?

   In your answer you should comment on:

   - the conditions in which the animals are kept;
   - the attitude of Janice, the kennel maid.

2   How does the writer make you feel sorry for the animals and for Wolf in particular?

   In your answer you should comment on:

   - the way Wolf and the other dogs are described;
   - the way the Carter family react;
   - why most people have not wanted to adopt Wolf;
   - how you think this story might end.

| HOMEWORK C22 | (25 MINUTES) |

Spend about five minutes reading the information about Auton Fells Animal Rescue Centre on the next page. Take no more than 20 minutes to answer this question.

1   What are the hidden messages in this Information Sheet about the Rescue Centre?

   In your answer you should consider:

   - how much the leaflet is appealing for funds;
   - how the writer may have have used emotive language to persuade the reader;
   - what the details about adopting a cat or dog are really saying;
   - how morally right it is to spend so much caring for donkeys when there are children in the world dying of starvation.

Auton Fells Animal Rescue Centre

Auton Fells was the home of the Cranton Family for many generations. Lady Anne Cranton, who started the Rescue Centre some forty years ago, left the property to the Trust when she died in 1970 and since that time it has become one of the leading facilities of its kind in the North of England, with a staff of twenty-five trained and dedicated animal specialists. It is now entirely dependent on charitable contributions for its upkeep. Please support our work. Your donation, no matter how small, will be appreciated.

Victims of the Sea

Much of the work of the Centre is devoted to treating seabirds such as razorbills and guillemots affected by oil in the sea. Increasingly swans, geese and ducks are being threatened by oil on inland waterways and are brought in for specialist cleaning.

Adopting an Animal from Auton Fells

Every year more than five hundred dogs and cats are brought to the centre, mostly unwanted pets. Often insufficient thought has been given to the purchase of the animal in the first place. They have been given as 'living toys' to children who tire of them, or they have not been properly trained and are then considered dirty or unruly.

Auton Fells tries to find good homes for all its animals. If you wish to adopt a cat or dog, please talk to one of our staff, and fill in the necessary forms. Within a week we will arrange for our Home Visiting Co-ordinator to meet you in your own home to discuss the details of caring for the animal of your choice and to assess your suitability.

Charges for the animals (£70 for dogs, £30 for cats) include neutering, identichipping, vaccination, de-fleaing and worming. As the adopter you will be responsible for all future veterinary bills, which can be very expensive.

Visiting Auton Fells

The Visitors' Centre is open daily from 10am to 3.30pm. Parties are welcome but we would appreciate notice in order that staff may be made available to show you around. For obvious reasons the Wild Birds Hospital is not open to the general public.

Donkey Sanctuary

The Lady Anne Donkey Sanctuary has rescued over four thousand donkeys since it was started. Often

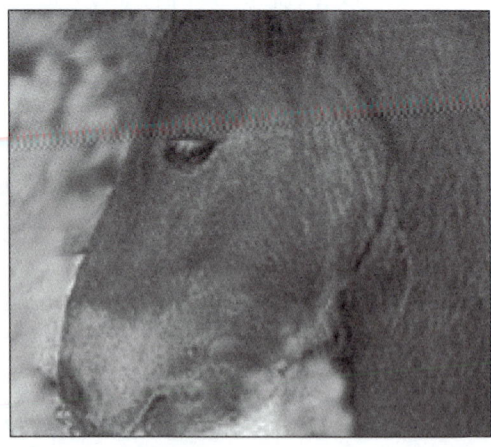

these poor animals are found in deplorable conditions, both in this country and abroad, too old to work, neglected and often cruelly treated. Auton Fells provides a safe environment for these loving and faithful creatures to live out their final days. At the present time we have over 200 donkeys in our fields and stables. Sadly the costs of this are enormous, over £1200.00 per year for each donkey.

Please support this very worthwhile cause.

These three homeworks are also designed to test your writing.

Spend about 40 minutes on each task and remember that you will be assessed on:

- your ideas and the way you organise and express them;
- your ability to write clearly, use paragraphs, punctuation, spelling and grammar.

HOMEWORK C23 (40 MINUTES)

Imagine that you are a Home Visiting Coordinator, working for an Animal Rescue Centre.

Write a report giving details of a visit you have made and giving the reasons why you are not able to recommend this adoption.

You may include details of the home conditions and what was actually said in the interview in reply to your questions which led to your final conclusions.

HOMEWORK C24 (40 MINUTES)

Write about an incident of cruelty to an animal.

You could:

- write about a real or imaginary event;
- write in the first person (as the animal) or in the third person.

HOMEWORK C25

Write a newspaper article entitled "A pet is for Life - not just for Christmas".

You could:

- try to persuade people to consider all the implications of owning a pet;
- give examples of suffering caused by people who buy animals without giving it enough thought.

OLIVER RUNS AWAY

This extract is from "Oliver Twist" by Charles Dickens. The young orphan, Oliver, has found life working for Sowerberry, the Undertaker, quite unbearable and has decided to run away.

It was eight o'clock now. Though he was nearly five miles away from the town, he ran, and hid behind the hedges, by turns, till noon, fearing that he might be pursued and overtaken. Then he sat down by the side of the milestone, and began to think, for the first time, where he had better go and try to live.

The stone by which he was seated, bore, in large characters, an intimation that it was just seventy miles from that spot to London. The name awakened a new train of ideas in the boy's mind. London! - that great large place! - nobody - not even Mr. Bumble - could ever find him there! He had often heard the old men in the workhouse, too, say that no lad of spirit need want in London; and that there were ways of living in that vast city, which those who had been bred up in country parts had no idea of. It was the very place for a homeless boy, who must die in the streets unless some one helped him. As these things passed through his thoughts, he jumped upon his feet, and again walked forward.

He had diminished the distance between himself and London by full four miles more, before he recollected how much he must undergo ere he could hope to reach his place of destination. As his consideration forced itself upon him, he slackened his pace a little, and meditated upon his means of getting there. He had a crust of bread, a coarse shirt, and two pairs of stockings, in his bundle. He had a penny too - a gift of Sowerberry's after some funeral in which he had acquitted himself more than ordinarily well - in his pocket.

"A clean shirt," thought Oliver, "is a very comfortable thing, very; and so are two pairs of darned stockings; and so is a penny; but they are small helps to a sixty-five miles' walk in winter-time."

But Oliver's thoughts, like those of most other people, although they were extremely ready and active to point out his difficulties, were wholly at a loss to suggest any feasible mode of surmounting them; so, after a good deal of thinking to no particular purpose, he changed his little bundle over to the other shoulder, and trudged on.

Oliver walked twenty miles that day; and all that time tasted nothing but the crust of dry bread, and a few draughts of water, which he begged at the cottage doors by the roadside. When the night came, he turned into a meadow; and, creeping close under a hay-rick, determined to lie there, till morning. He felt frightened at first, for the wind moaned dismally over the empty fields; and he was cold and hungry, and more alone than he had ever felt before. Being very tired with his walk, however, he soon fell asleep and forgot his troubles.

He felt cold and stiff, when he got up the next morning, and so hungry that he was obliged to exchange the penny for a small loaf, in the very first village through which he passed. He had walked no more than twelve miles, when night closed in again. His feet were sore, and his legs so weak that they trembled beneath him. Another night passed in the bleak, damp air, made him worse; when he set forward on his journey the next morning, he could hardly crawl along.

He waited at the bottom of a steep hill till a stage-coach came up, and then begged of the outside passengers; but there were very few who took any notice of him; and even those told him to wait till they got to the top of the hill, and then let them see how far he could run for a halfpenny. Poor Oliver tried to keep up with the coach a little way, but was unable to do it, by reason of his fatigue and sore feet. When the outsides saw this, they put their halfpence back into their pockets again, declaring that he was an idle young dog, and didn't deserve anything; and the coach rattled away and left only a cloud of dust behind.

In some villages, large painted boards were fixed up, warning all persons who begged within the district, that they would be sent to jail. This frightened Oliver very much, and made him glad to get out of these villages with all possible expedition. In others he would stand about the inn-yards, and look mournfully at every one who passed, a proceeding which generally terminated in the landlady's ordering one of the post-boys who were lounging about, to drive that strange boy out of the place, for she was sure he had come to steal something. If he begged at a farmer's house, ten to one but they threatened to set the dog on him; and when he showed his nose in a shop, they talked about the beadle - which brought Oliver's heart into his mouth - very often the only thing he had there, for many hours together.

In fact, if it had not been for a good-hearted turnpike-man, and a benevolent old lady, Oliver's troubles would have been shortened by the very same process which had put an end to his mother's; in other words, he would most assuredly have fallen dead upon the king's highway. But the turnpike-man gave him a meal of bread and cheese; and the old lady, who had a shipwrecked grandson wandering barefoot in some distant part of the earth, took pity upon the poor orphan, and gave him what little she could afford - and more - with such kind and gentle words, and such tears of sympathy and compassion, that they sank deeper into Oliver's soul, than all the sufferings he had ever undergone.

Early on the seventh morning after he had left his native place, Oliver limped slowly into the little town of Barnet. The window shutters were closed; the street was empty; not a soul had awakened to the business of the day. The sun was rising in all its splendid beauty; but the light only served to show the boy his own lonesomeness and desolation, as he sat, with bleeding feet and covered with dust, upon a doorstep.

By degrees, the shutters were opened; the window blinds were drawn up; and people began passing to and fro. Some few stopped to gaze at Oliver for a moment or two, or turned round to stare at him as they hurried by; but none relieved him, or troubled themselves to inquire how he came there. He had no heart to beg. And there he sat.

HOMEWORK C26 (40 MINUTES)

You should be used to working within time limits, and using every minute of the time allowed.

Do not forget to refer to words and phrases in the passage to support your ideas.

The time allowed for this homework is 40 minutes.

1. What qualities does Oliver show in this part of the story?

    In your answer you should comment on:

    - the things which he does and his reactions to things which are done to him;
    - his reaction to and thoughts about the other characters in the story.

2. How does Dickens describe Oliver to make you feel increasingly sorry for him?

    In your answer you should comment on:

    - the sequence of events;
    - the words that are actually used to describe Oliver;
    - the social conditions of that time in history;
    - the way in which people in this extract treat Oliver.

HOMEWORK C27 (25 MINUTES)

Spend about five minutes reading the information about Homelessness on the next page.

Take no more than 20 minutes to answer this question.

1. For whom do you think this Factsheet about Homelessness has been written?

    In your answer you should comment on:

    - how much of what is written is directed towards homeless people themselves and how much towards a reader with a general interest in the subject;
    - what leads you to the conclusions you have just made;
    - the way facts and figures are combined with some personal and emotive comments from homeless people;
    - what purpose, if any, you think such a sheet might serve.

THE PLIGHT OF THE HOMELESS

The number of people sleeping rough in England tonight will be between 8,000 and 10,000.

HOMELESSNESS - WHAT IS IT?

We use this term to describe any person without a legal right to a roof over their head. It includes people who are forced to live in insecure, illegal, overcrowded, dangerous, or very temporary accommodation - i.e. hostels, women's refuges and squats.

DANNY'S STORY

Danny is just sixteen. He ran away from home four months ago, for reasons which he says he cannot talk about. He ended up in London and is living and sleeping on the streets. The little money he had is long gone. At first he says he was full of hope and thought he would get a job and a flat. Now he has given up trying and he sits around on street corners all day wrapped in a dirty, old blanket. He told me, "People look at me like I'm rubbish. I suppose I am really."

HEALTH CARE

People living on the streets or in various kinds of temporary accommodation and those on low incomes, are more prone to illnesses and infections. Many people feel that they cannot register with a doctor because they do not have an address, or perhaps because they do not know their NHS number. This is not true. Neither of these should prevent a person from registering with a surgery or health centre which may be able to offer help in a variety of ways, not just in preventing or treating illness.

THE RESEARCH

Research shows that in large urban areas (towns and cities with a population of over 250,000) there are over 140,000 people aged from 16 to 25 who are homeless.

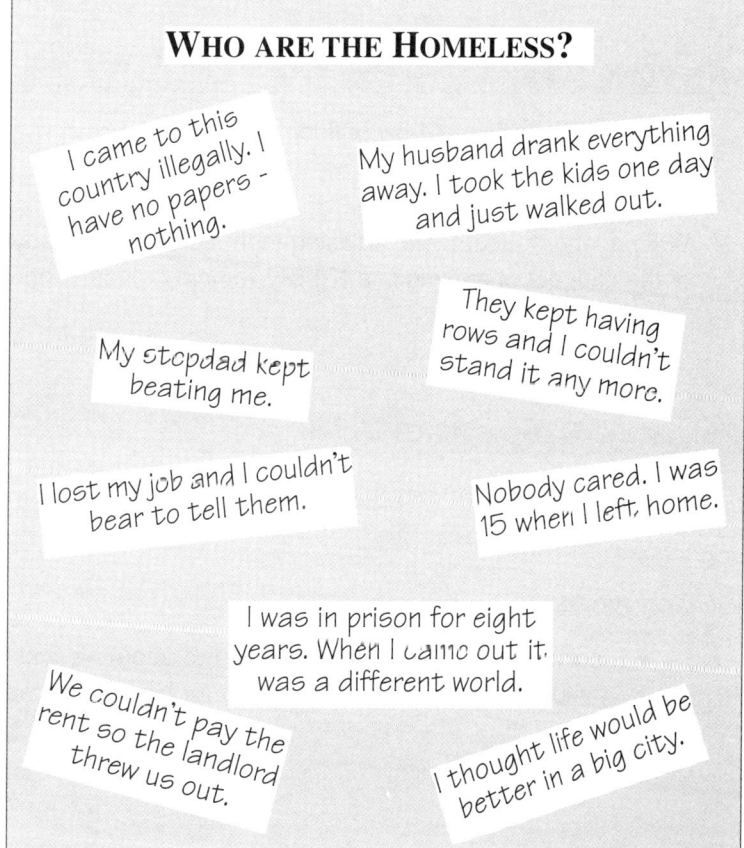

WHO ARE THE HOMELESS?

I came to this country illegally. I have no papers - nothing.

My husband drank everything away. I took the kids one day and just walked out.

My stepdad kept beating me.

They kept having rows and I couldn't stand it any more.

I lost my job and I couldn't bear to tell them.

Nobody cared. I was 15 when I left home.

I was in prison for eight years. When I came out it was a different world.

We couldn't pay the rent so the landlord threw us out.

I thought life would be better in a big city.

WHAT IS BEING DONE?

There is someone out there willing to listen and help if you know where to look.

The YMCA (Young Men's Christian Association) is an organisation which provides some 6,500 bedspaces per night in Britain in a variety of projects - hostels, flats, bedsits, foyers, Nightstops. Other programmes include Outreach, detached youth and community work, training and support, and rehousing for young people in Young Offenders Units. They may be found in the Business Section of Phone Books under Y.

Spend about 40 minutes on each of the three final writing tasks on this page.

As you write remember that you will be assessed on a number of things:

- your ideas and the way you organise and express them;
- your ability to write clearly, use paragraphs, punctuation, spelling and grammar;
- handwriting and presentation do make a difference to the first impression your work will have on an examiner.

HOMEWORK C28

Imagine a close friend has confided in you that he or she is going to run away from home.

Write a letter to that friend advising them against doing anything in a hurry and warning them of the dangers of arriving in a big city without friends, money or anywhere to live.

HOMEWORK C29

Write about a modern-day Oliver and the night that he arrives in London, or some other city.

You should:

- include as much detail as time allows about his first impressions of the city;
- try to create a feeling of sympathy for him by describing his feelings.

HOMEWORK C30

Write a newspaper article explaining why you think that more should be done to help the enormous number of people in this country who are homeless, for whatever reasons.

You could:

- include imaginary interviews with homeless people;
- make suggestions as to how you think we could all help with this problem.

BRAINTRAINS

HOMEWORK B1   **TREASURE HUNT**

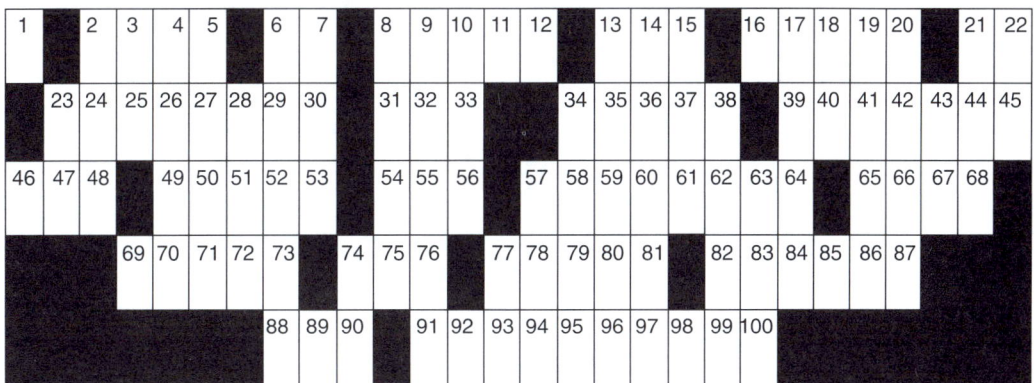

You can find answers to these clues in the Reference Section of your library

Each clue will give you a letter and the numbers of any boxes where that letter fits.

1. The wife of the Greek philosopher, Socrates. 1st letter gives 92.
2. Make of the car nicknamed "The Beetle". 1st letter gives 4.
3. He discovered Newfoundland and Nova Scotia. 1st letter gives 72 & 99.
4. He wrote 'Brighton Rock'. 1st letter of surname gives 26, 53, 57.
5. Inventor of the microscope. 1st of surname gives 65.
6. Part of the throat containing the vocal chords. 1st letter gives 2, 23, 34, 38.
7. The 1900 Olympic Games were held in this city. 1st letter for 83 & 93.
8. The rupee is the currency of this country. 1st for 41, 71, 84, 86, 96.
9. Nickname of New Zealand Rugby League tourists. 1st for 11.
10. Official language of Pakistan. 1st gives 18, 25, 78.
11. Writer of the musical 'Oliver!' 1st of surname for 8.
12. Element with the symbol Sn. 1st for 13, 28, 54, 61 64, 74, 87.
13. Tangiers is a port in this country. 1st for 50, 79, 88.
14. Nationality of the composer Sibelius. 1st for 7, 22, 39.
15. President of USA 1933-45. 1st of surname for 30, 40, 47, 58, 85, 95.
16. This county lies to the east of Lancashire. 1st for 36, 67, 90.
17. English poet married to Sylvia Plath. 1st of surname for 14, 27, 55, 70, 73, 75, 77.
18. Caviare is made from the eggs of this fish. 1st for 12, 16, 45, 63, 68, 82.
19. World's longest river. 1st for 19, 32, 43, 52, 81, 98.
20. Thomas Hardy's county. 1st for 20, 33, 44.
21. Largest city in New Zealand. 1st for 1, 24, 31, 37, 46, 49, 60, 80, 89.
22. Prime Minister of Britain 1951 - 1955. 1st of first name for 69.
23. Author of 'The Road to Wigan Pier'. 1st of surname for 3, 6, 9, 10, 17, 21, 35, 51, 66.
24. Biological term - outer part of skin. 1st for 5, 15, 29, 42, 48, 56, 59, 62, 76, 91, 94, 97, 100.

HOMEWORK B2 — CROSSWORD

Clues Across

1. Oh! Catches role to assist learning. (Anag) (13)
8. Poor girl fell through her mirror. (5)
9. Dawn. (5)
10. Of the nose. (5)
11. Testing times abbreviated. (5)
13. Throw out. (5)
15. Verse. (6)
16. Miss Capulet of Verona. (6)
18. Extra! Extra! (5)
21. Spanish courtyard. (5)
23. Prefix among or between. (5)
24. Author of 'The Mill on the Floss'. (5)
25. Looking for inspiration? Ask Sadie. (Anag.) (5)
26. In the direction of an adverb. (13)

Clues Down

1. Adjective describing 1564 - 1616. (13)
2. Major port, N. Israel. (5)
3. Signs of the future. (5)
4. Past, present or future? (6)
5. Where Elisa the bride might walk. (Anag.) (5)
6. Indian language. (5)
7. Again and again and again! (13)
12. Should be found in 15 Across. (5)
14. Ancient Roman house. (15)
17. Not passive. (6)
19. Comparatively arid. (5)
20. Drainage channel. (5)
21. Thanks Mr Caxton for this. (5)
22. 3 pl. Possessive adjective. (5)

Endpapers: Looking down into a television studio through a forest of lights slung from the ceiling. These lights, which include 'barndoors', 'floods' and 'spots', are mounted on tracks and can be moved by remote control from the studio floor to create different lighting effects.

SEE INSIDE
A TELEVISION STUDIO

SERIES EDITOR
R.J. UNSTEAD

HUTCHINSON OF LONDON

Series Editor
R. J. Unstead

Author
George Beal

Illustrations
John Berry, John Marshall
Tudor Art

Published by Hutchinson & Co (Publishers) Ltd
3 Fitzroy Square, London W1
London Melbourne Sydney Auckland Wellington
Johannesburg and agencies throughout the world

First published 1977

Designed and Produced by Grisewood & Dempsey Ltd
Elsley House, 24 Great Titchfield Street, London W1

ISBN 0 09 131490 9

© Grisewood & Dempsey Ltd 1977

Printed in Great Britain by W. S. Cowell Ltd
Ipswich, Suffolk

CONTENTS

People Behind the Camera	8
The Control Room	10
How the Camera Works	12
Recording Equipment	14
Televising a Play	16
How a Show is Produced	18
'Here is the News'	20
Travelling Studio	22
Special Effects and Props	24
Television by Satellite	26
The Story of Television	27
Glossary of Terms	28
Index	29

The editors wish to thank Mr. David Bull, Head of Cameras at the BBC, Anglia Television Ltd., Granada Television Ltd., and Mr Alan Hawkins, Studio Supervisor at ITN, for their assistance in the preparation of this book.

Electronic Miracle

On 30 September, 1929, the world's first television broadcast took place. It was an experimental transmission by the BBC, and it lasted for only two minutes. There was no sound, which was broadcast later, but John Logie Baird, the inventor, was very pleased to know that at last, a real television transmission had taken place – even though only 29 television receivers were in existence. A crude, 30-line experimental system was used for tests three years later, but in 1936, television broadcasting began in earnest. The BBC, using a 405-line system, had begun regular transmissions. But there were still only about 400 receivers, and even they had to be used within 30 miles of the transmitter.

Today, television has become part of the lives of people the world over. In Britain alone, the average television set is turned on for more than five hours each day.

It is a miracle of electronic engineering, invented by a series of men over a period of almost a hundred years. A century ago, there was no television, no radio. Although the art of photography was in its early stages, there was no cinema, although the telephone and the talking machine had just appeared on the scene. The transformation of that scene in one hundred years has been truly miraculous. And what of the future? How will television develop? It seems likely that the television of the future will probably be piped by cable into our homes. It will probably have a very large screen, and we shall almost certainly possess our own video-tape machine for showing programmes at will.

Left: 'On location'. A cameraman on camelback filming in the desert. Right: A studio's sound control room. Through the glass panel is the control room where the picture is monitored at the same time.

People behind the Camera

When we see the television screen showing a picture of just one person – say, someone reading the News – we tend to forget that a whole team of people is necessary, just to transmit that single person's image. Some of the members of the team are shown on this page, but there are plenty of others. For instance, there are the programme researchers, who make sure that the facts of the programme are correct; the graphics team, who provide the words, diagrams and models; the wardrobe department, which supplies all the costumes; and a floor manager, whose job it is to see that everyone knows just what is happening, and who keeps the whole range of activities working smoothly. Apart from these, there are carpenters, electricians, painters and others, whose jobs may not seem glamorous, but who are essential, all the same.

MAKING UP FOR TV
For 'straight' parts, such as interviews, and so on, very little make-up is needed, if any. But for character roles, all kinds of materials are used. Faces are remodelled by using putty, wax or collodion. Sheets of plastic add bulk or folds to a face, while scars, cuts and bruises can be applied, cut-to-size and made-to-measure! Property 'hair' makes wigs, moustaches, beards, and so on.

THE SET
This is built from wood, hardboard and hessian, and then painted.

CAMERA
Camera operators must position their cameras correctly, use the right lens, and keep the subject in focus.

LIGHTING
Much time is spent in getting the lighting correct, with the right power, and proper positioning.

SOUND CONTROL
Microphones are placed so as to pick up sound clearly. Some are fixed, and some are on long movable rods or booms.

VIDEO-TAPE
Most programmes are recorded on tape, and can be edited.

MAKE-UP
Make-up artists use all sorts of paints, powders and liquids; even special putties and plastics.

PRODUCTION
The producer of a programme is in overall charge.

DIRECTION
The director controls and interprets the programme as it proceeds.

Studio Activities

In the course of a day's broadcasting, a busy television station sends out a large number of quite different types of programmes. Some are 'live': that is, they are produced in the studio, and televised as they happen; while others are recorded, either on film or on video-tape. Some programmes come from outside the studio, such as outside broadcasts of sports events or from theatres and concert-halls. Television stations are linked with others in the same country, so that programmes can be *networked*. This means

Outside broadcasts, particularly for such events as sports, are linked to the studio by land line, or, for longer distances, by VHF radio.

News programmes are usually a mixture of live transmission from the studio, video-tape and film material, carefully edited together.

Feature films form an important part of a studio's programme, and are televised by using a telecine machine, turning film into TV.

Plays are usually recorded on video-tape, which means that any mistakes or failures can be re-shot and edited in to the programme.

Ten seconds to transmission. In the semi-darkness of the control room a red light glows under the monitor screen linked to camera one in the studio. Another production is about to go out. The control room is the nerve centre of a television studio. Here the chaotic variety of activity is directed with split-second timing.

Many stations are supported by advertising. The advertisements are supplied to the station, which 'slots' them in at the agreed time.

Sometimes, a 'hook-up' is arranged with other studios, and combined programmes are made, showing several scenes all in one picture.

that a popular programme can be seen by viewers everywhere. Of course, there are some programmes which are local only, such as weather reports. All these different productions need to be carefully planned and timed so that they fit neatly into the day's televising schedules. It is not simply a question of putting on one programme after another: the control room monitors the length of transmissions, while the next item is got ready. This may be an advertising, publicity or information 'slot', but split-second timing is essential. Programmes can also sometimes be interrupted for important news items which can be 'flashed' in.

TELEVISION PROMPTER

Have you ever wondered how people on television remember everything they have to say? Of course, actors and such performers learn a script in advance, but in news programmes and similar broadcasts, this is just not possible. The simplest answer is for someone to hold up a board (out of sight of the camera) with the words written on it. A better system uses an endless strip of wide paper which winds on to rollers. The words are printed on the roll. Another system has the message appearing on a small 'monitor' screen just below the camera.

The Control Room

The control room is the hub of the television studio. In front of the control room staff are rows of monitor screens, which can be 40 or more – or fewer – according to the needs of the programme being transmitted. The staff of the control room consists of the director of the programme; the production assistant; the vision mixer; the technical liaison manager; and the vision operator. Behind a sound-proof glass panel is the sound control room, staffed by the sound supervisor and his engineers.

What we are seeing in this control room is the transmission of a television play (see pages 16–17), and each of the monitor screens is showing some part or viewpoint of the programme. In overall command is the director, seen in the foreground, with his production assistant and the vision mixer. All three are concerned with the bank of monitors on the left. The technical manager and the vision operator work from the screens at the far end. The production assistant works in advance of the director, calling the camera shots before they are due, and following the script carefully. As the director gives his orders, such as 'Cut to camera 3', the vision mixer operates her controls to change the shots. Meanwhile, the technical manager watches the next shot due to go up, to make sure that the circuits are working properly, while the vision operator is checking the colour and black and white electronic levels.

All the microphones are connected to the sound control room, where the engineers have their own monitor screens. Dozens of microphones are in use, and the sound can be adjusted very expertly, and special effects can be fed in, such as echoes or deadening of sounds. The vision controller can change the colour balance, and he can also transmit any shot to any one of the small monitors on the back of the television cameras. The lighting director is in control of all the lights in the studio, and has his own operator in the control room.

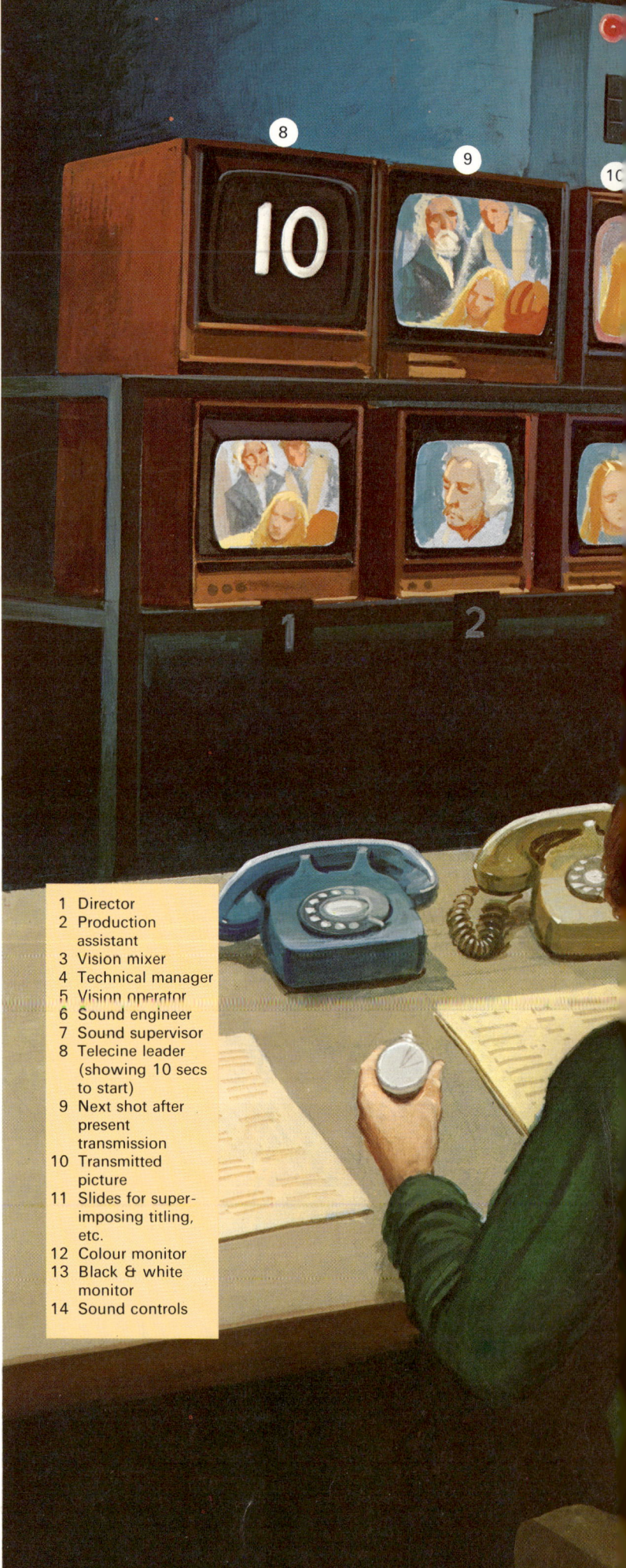

1 Director
2 Production assistant
3 Vision mixer
4 Technical manager
5 Vision operator
6 Sound engineer
7 Sound supervisor
8 Telecine leader (showing 10 secs to start)
9 Next shot after present transmission
10 Transmitted picture
11 Slides for super-imposing titling, etc.
12 Colour monitor
13 Black & white monitor
14 Sound controls

How the Camera Works

What we think of as white light is made up of many colours, but we can think of them as three primary ones – red, green and blue. Colour cameras are made to distinguish these colours. The light passes through the lens, and first reaches a coloured mirror called a *dichroic mirror*. This one is blue, and it reflects the blue light through the mirror on to a lens, and then to a camera tube. Red and green light pass through, and strike a red dichroic mirror. The green light passes through, and reaches a second camera tube. The red light is reflected by the red dichroic mirror, through a lens, on to a third camera tube. So we have three images focused, one on each colour tube. In black and white television, only one camera tube is used. Inside the camera, the light is focused on to the face of the camera tube (three tubes for a colour camera). These tube faces are coated on the inside with a light-sensitive material which charges electrically in proportion to the amount of light falling on it. This coating is 'scanned' by an electron beam focused on to it from an electron gun at the other end of the tube; the electron beam cancels the charge in the coating, and converts it into an electrical signal which is the output of the tube. It is these three tube out-

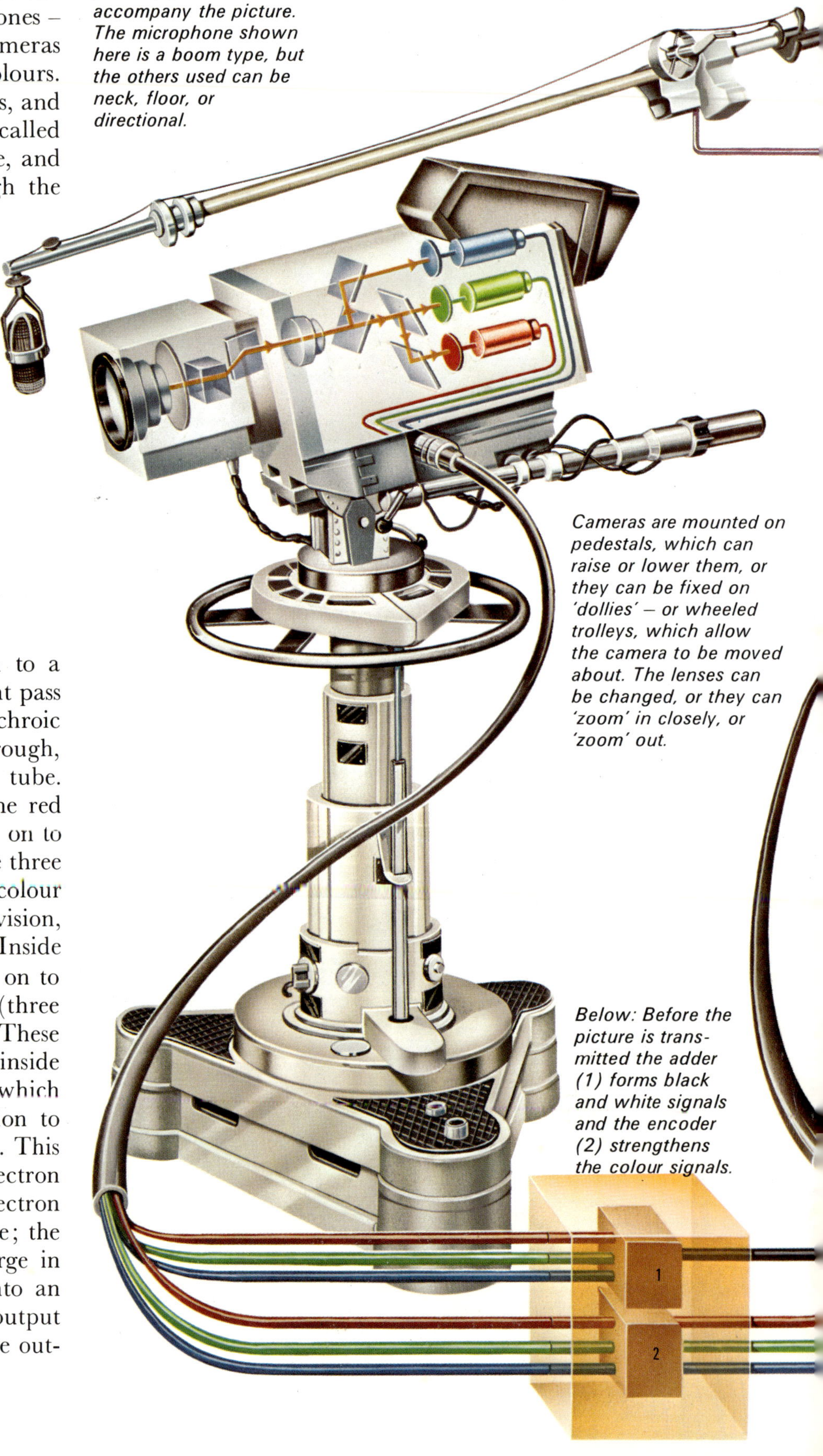

The studio microphone picks up the sound to accompany the picture. The microphone shown here is a boom type, but the others used can be neck, floor, or directional.

Cameras are mounted on pedestals, which can raise or lower them, or they can be fixed on 'dollies' – or wheeled trolleys, which allow the camera to be moved about. The lenses can be changed, or they can 'zoom' in closely, or 'zoom' out.

Below: Before the picture is transmitted the adder (1) forms black and white signals and the encoder (2) strengthens the colour signals.

puts, combined together, that make up the colour picture.

Every colour receiver has three electron guns (one for each colour), and all fire their stream of electrons at the screen at the end of the tube. This screen is covered all over with tiny dots of phosphor, grouped in sets of three; one each for red, green and blue. As the 'guns' fire at the screen, the dots are 'lit up': the red dots by the red gun, the green dots by the green gun, and the blue dots by the blue gun. The electron beams 'scan' the tube sideways, and up and down, according to the line-standard used. For most of Europe, this is 625 lines. The signals from the TV cameras are relayed from the studio to the transmitter, together with the sound signals. These signals are picked up by viewers' aerials, and so on to the set.

Transmitters send out the signals for television on two carrier waves. The length of each 'wave' is called a wavelength, *and the number of waves sent out per second is called the* frequency. *These are measured in* Hertz.

Between the electron gun and the screen is the 'shadow' plate or mask. This mask contains thousands of tiny holes, and the combined red, green and blue signals go through each hole together, and hit the screen.

13

Recording Equipment

A great many programmes seen on television are from films or recordings. In fact, about half is film. This has to be converted into TV signals, and to do this, a *telecine* machine is used. The simplest one is called a vidicon crossfire machine, and is shown in the top diagram. Another system, which is less wearing on film, is called the flying-spot prism telecine, and this is shown below. One of the technical problems which is overcome is that ordinary film is shown at a rate of 24 frames a second, while TV uses 25. The sound track of film is either *optical* – looking like an irregular strip alongside the picture – or *striped*. This means that it has a track down the side of the film something like the tape of a tape recorder. In either case, the telecine machine has to pick up the sound, either by shining a lamp through the track on to a photo-electric cell, or by picking up the striped track with a playback head.

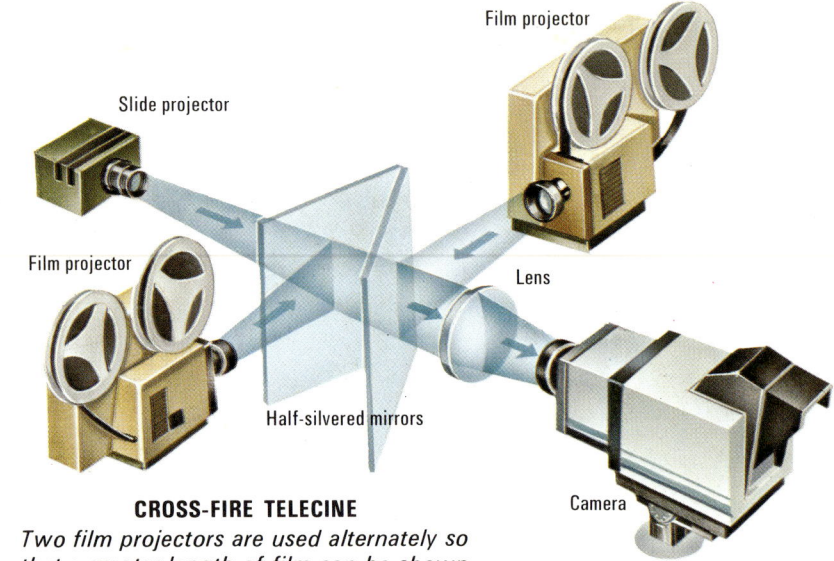

CROSS-FIRE TELECINE
Two film projectors are used alternately so that a greater length of film can be shown without interruption. Two half-silvered mirrors are placed in position. At this angle these reflect the projected film, like ordinary mirrors, at 90° into the camera. At the same time, slides of captions etc., can be projected through the mirrors at a non-reflective angle directly into the camera.

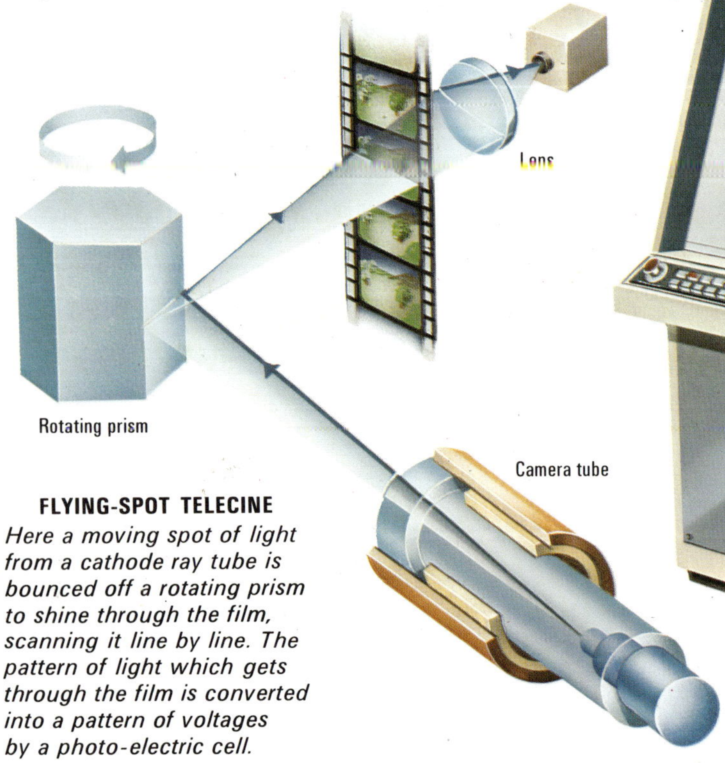

FLYING-SPOT TELECINE
Here a moving spot of light from a cathode ray tube is bounced off a rotating prism to shine through the film, scanning it line by line. The pattern of light which gets through the film is converted into a pattern of voltages by a photo-electric cell.

Television pictures can be recorded on magnetic tape. The machine used to do this is called a video-tape recorder (VTR). Variations in brightness along each line of a picture are changed into a varying electric current. This passes through a special rotating electromagnet called the recording head. It produces a magnetic pattern on a tape, which is drawn past

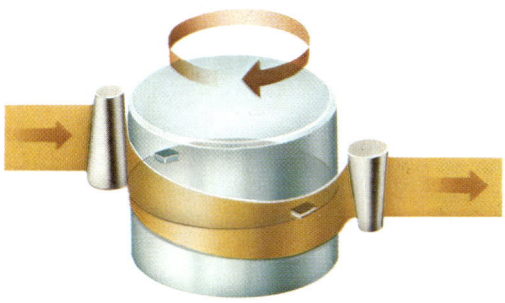

Above: Rotating head disc showing tape feeding through at an angle to make diagonal recording.

PORTABLE VIDEO-TAPE MACHINE
This looks very much like an ordinary tape-recorder, except that it uses wider tape and records both sound and vision.

the head. Because the head rotates, it records the vision signal in a series of narrow strips, diagonally across the tape. The total length of these strips is much longer than the tape itself. This arrangement is necessary in order to record faithfully the numerous brightness variations contained in a typical picture – if a video-tape recorder were made like an ordinary sound tape

Below: Diagram of video-tape showing recording angle.

recorder, the tape would have to pass the fixed recording head at about 30 metres a second in order to make a high quality recording. When the tape is played back, the rotating head picks up the recorded signal. This is used to make up the television picture. The recording can be erased when it is no longer required. The tape can then be used for another recording.

A hand-held video camera, like the one in the picture, is used with the portable video-tape machine. The tape is coated with iron oxide, which is magnetized, according to the strength of the signal. When it is played back, the recorder picks up the varying magnetism on the tape, turns it into an electric signal, which is passed to a television tube, (the receiver). This reproduces the original programme exactly.

For immediate playback of a scene a recording is usually made on a special magnetic video disc – similar to a gramophone record. On the screen above viewers can take a second look at a chick cracking open its egg while watching the same chick taking notice of its new world.

Televising a Play

Dramatic presentations on television can be films, they can be live plays, or video-taped beforehand. This last way is by far the most common, since there is little point in doing a play 'live'. Television films, of course, are more related to the cinema. A true television play is part and parcel of television, and is usually produced in the studio. A play starts with an idea. It may be specially written, or it may be adapted from a book or stage play. In any case, the first thing that must be done is to write a script.

Once the script is done, a conference is held to decide how the play is to be produced. Some rewriting will need to be done. There will be an editor, a producer, and a director. Perhaps there will be a casting director, too, who will be responsible for choosing and finding the right actors to play the parts. While this is going on, a designer will be working on ideas for the sets. He will make sketches and models, while the wardrobe department will be working on the costumes required. Once all these different departments have got to work, the actors will be called in, and rehearsals will start.

In this scene from a play, three cameras are being used. Each will 'see' a different view of the scene. The director, in the control room, will be able to choose which of the three shots he wishes. The floor manager, standing in front, has a monitor screen, which shows which shot is being televised.

In this 'period-piece' play, every detail must be carefully watched and checked — for instance, the furniture and costumes must be of the right period. The director in the control room can speak directly to the crew in the studio through their headsets.

17

How a Show is Produced

SCRIPT CONFERENCE
The writer, the editor and the producer meet to discuss the play.

CASTING
The director and the casting director choose actors for the parts.

BUILDING THE SET
From the designer's plans, the carpenters and painters set to work.

FINAL PRODUCTION
After much preparation, the play is performed before the cameras.

WARDROBE
The studio wardrobe supplies costumes or has them made to fit.

Although most of the action in a television play is staged in the studio, outdoor scenes have to be done on location, perhaps using film. Location scenes are expensive, so all the outdoor work is done at the same time. Later, these scenes will be edited into the main play in the correct sequence. When all the studio work has been finished, the director runs the whole play through to see that the video-taping has been done correctly. At this stage he may decide to edit out, or change some scenes. The same kind of care is taken with all television productions, whether they are plays, comedy shows, light entertainment, or documentaries. Commercials are produced outside the studios, but the same standards are employed. Complicated sets are not absolutely necessary, for it is possible to obtain many effects quite simply.

> **CHILDREN'S TELEVISION**
> Most countries now produce special television programmes for children. In fact, some of the most popular programmes of all have been made for children, but adults have shown equal interest! Television is particularly suitable for puppet shows or cartoons, but some of the best drama has first been shown on children's television. Apart from purely entertainment programmes, television has been used widely for educational purposes.

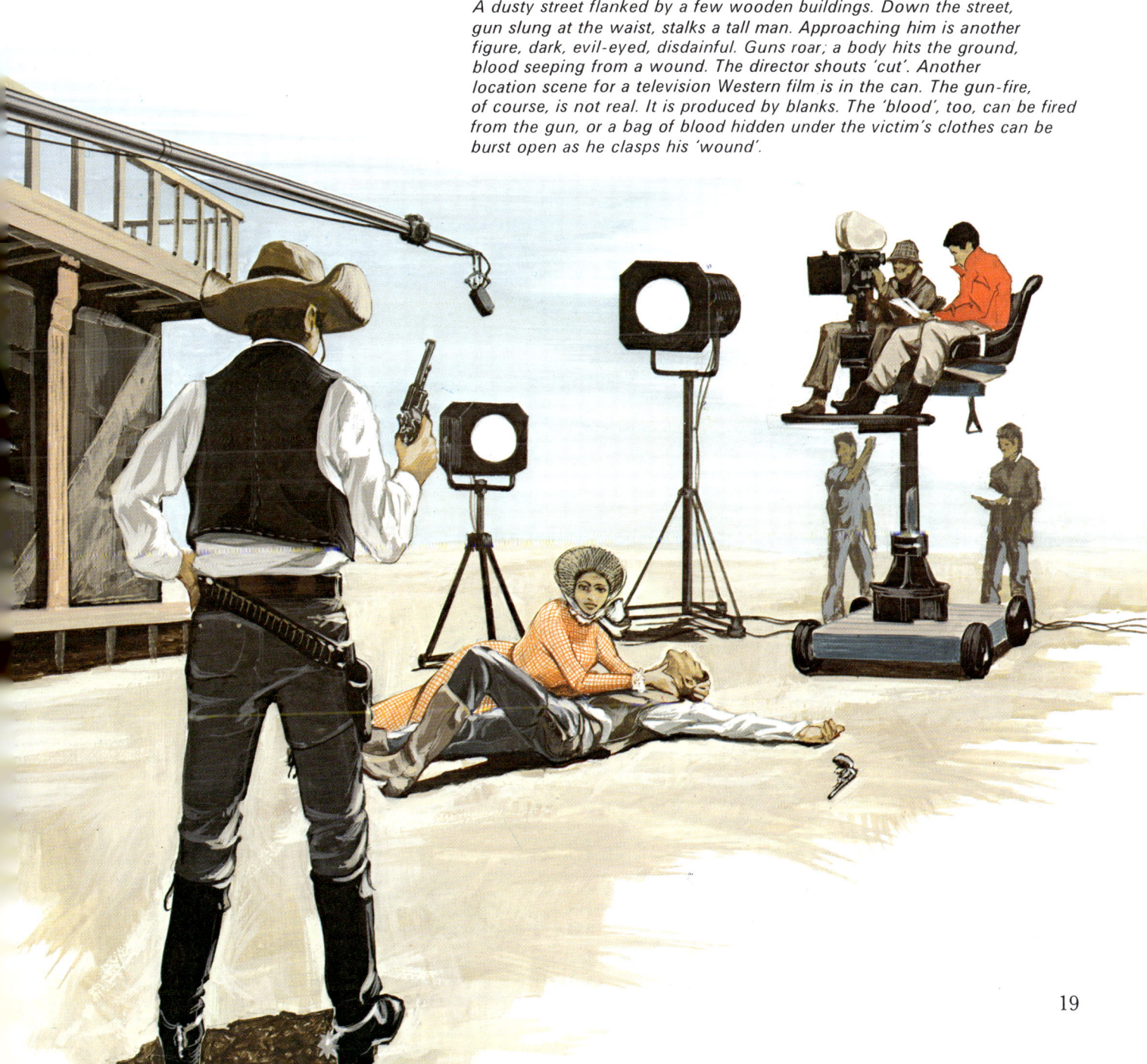

A dusty street flanked by a few wooden buildings. Down the street, gun slung at the waist, stalks a tall man. Approaching him is another figure, dark, evil-eyed, disdainful. Guns roar; a body hits the ground, blood seeping from a wound. The director shouts 'cut'. Another location scene for a television Western film is in the can. The gun-fire, of course, is not real. It is produced by blanks. The 'blood', too, can be fired from the gun, or a bag of blood hidden under the victim's clothes can be burst open as he clasps his 'wound'.

Reporting teams use any possible means to get their story and pictures. The crew on the left is shooting a scene with a 16 mm film camera from a helicopter flying over the sea where an oil tanker has been involved in a collision.

Right: A typical scene in a television news studio. The newscasters sit at their desk with their scripts in front of them. Beyond is the battery of cameras and other equipment. Special cameras are used so that the newscasters' heads can be shown superimposed on the picture itself. A news sequence might contain sections of film, video-tape, captions or still photographs.

'Here is the News'

All television transmissions are the result of team effort, none more so than television news. The faces we see most on the television news programmes are the newscasters, who very often, have a background of newspaper-reporting. They need to be confident, friendly and fluent readers. Backing them up in the studio is a team of professional newsmen and women, much as one would find on a newspaper.

Outside the studio, are the television reporters, who cover the world to supply an up-to-the minute service to the news broadcasts. A reporting team needs at least one cameraman, a sound recordist and a lighting engineer, apart from the reporter. Film is normally used; and once the spools have been exposed, the cans are rushed back to the studio by a dispatch rider, to be processed immediately. Overseas assignments mean getting the film to some convenient place where, once processed, it can be transmitted via satellite to the home studio. Television news studios have staff men stationed all over the country, and at important places abroad, and it is these men who help the editor decide what events shall be covered during a day. Other news comes in from agencies and free-lance newsmen, and there is constant interchange of information between the television news services of the various countries across the world.

Every day, as on a newspaper, television news services hold a morning conference, which is attended by the news editor, the foreign editor, the chief sub-editor and other executives, under the leadership of the editor. Decisions are made, the conference breaks up, and camera teams and reporting crews are sent out on their assignments.

Later on, when the news bulletin goes on the air, the director works out how the various items shall appear. A newsreader reads out a section, the director cuts to a piece of film or a live report from an outside broadcast.

Each of the newscasters has his own small monitor in front of him, so that he can see which picture is being transmitted. In the scene on the right, camera one has a red light, which shows that it is transmitting, while the newscaster has his own personal red light just below his monitor. A digital clock helps him time his reading accurately. The scripts are read partly from an autocue, which means that the newscaster can look at the camera as he speaks. We can see the girl operator on the right, rolling the script through the autocue machine by hand. This is picked up by the autocue camera placed above it, and the signal is carried by cable to the front of the cameras, where the script is reflected into a mirror.

Travelling Studio

Although most of the programmes seen on television are produced, or are televised from the studio, there are many important events or spectacles which can only be broadcast by sending teams out of the studio, to work on the spot. Sporting events are the most usual, but such occasions of world wide interest as the Silver Jubilee of Queen Elizabeth II in 1977 can obviously only be shot on the spot. It can, of course, be filmed, but this is not normally the function of a TV team which specializes in outside broadcasts. Special mobile cameras and mobile studios are used, and programmes are transmitted back to the main studio by cables, or by microwave radio links.

The mobile studio is housed in a specially equipped van, which is truly a miniature studio and control room. It is from this centre that the various cameras and sound units on the outside broadcast scene are controlled. The producer, sound engineers and vision controllers work inside the van very much as they would do back in the studio, but on a smaller scale, of course. Not all outside broadcasts are televised in the open air. It may be necessary to work inside a building, such as a church or a theatre; in which case special studio lighting has to be provided.

An outside broadcast commentator usually has a specially equipped position, such as a 'box' at a football match, placed in a good vantage point in the stand. Here, he will have his own monitor screens, so that he can watch the scene as it is picked up by each camera at any moment.

Above is the large van housing the control centre. Such vans are referred to as 'scanners', and this one is shown cut-away to reveal the operations centre inside.

Outside broadcast units carry their own captioning machines (above), so that the scores can be superimposed on the picture.

Left: A typical outside broadcast — a show-jumping event. Three cameras are trained on the arena, each able to transmit a picture from a different viewpoint. A zoom lens can be used to bring a distant scene into close-up, without the necessity for changing lenses or refocusing. The cameras are linked by cable to the commentator, who has monitor screens, a prompt book for following the events, and a hand microphone. He is also connected to the mobile control centre, from which the producer can speak to him, over the earphones.

Special Effects and Props

Have you ever wondered why, when a television actor falls through a window, he doesn't cut himself? It's because the 'glass' isn't real glass, but a plastic called C-2. Flames are produced by a special chemical; while 'blood' is a mixture of glycerine and colour produced by the make-up department. Those heavy-looking brick walls which collapse are usually made of painted plastic foam, while chairs smashed in television fights are really made of light balsa-wood.

Below: The same scene may be drawn from different distances and angles, and used as a background in a series such as a puppet show.

It is quite easy to fake the driving of a car in the studio. A back-projection moving picture of the required scene is set up behind the car. The car itself is placed on a movable platform so that the vehicle can be rocked slightly. The driver moves the steering wheel, a wind is added by means of a fan, and the whole scene is filmed or video-taped. The result is what appears to be a car driving along a country road.

'Fog' is produced by mixing a chemical with water and heating it, or by heating solid frozen carbon dioxide. 'Snow' is light flakes of plastic, or even soap flakes, blown through a wind machine – something like a giant electric fan.

Opposite page (top): A city blazes. Not a real one, of course, but a life-like miniature made by the studio's model-makers. The simple raw materials they use include cardboard, cotton wool, putty and paint. Just in case the fire gets out of control there is a one-man fire brigade at the ready with an extinguisher.

THE 'PROPS' PEOPLE

Properties or 'props' are all the hundreds of items needed on the set of a television show, ranging from a cigarette lighter to a double-decker bus. It is the job of the property department – the 'props' people – to find and supply such things. If it is a period play, the plot may need an old newspaper – or an unusual animal; maybe a camel or an armadillo. Telephones, toys, cars or cameras; these are all 'props'.

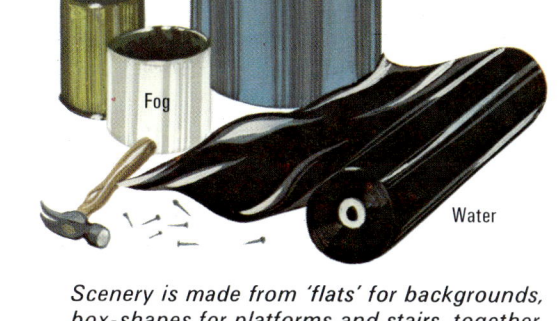

Scenery is made from 'flats' for backgrounds, box-shapes for platforms and stairs, together with cylinders and other geometrical shapes. These, with sculptured pieces, are painted.

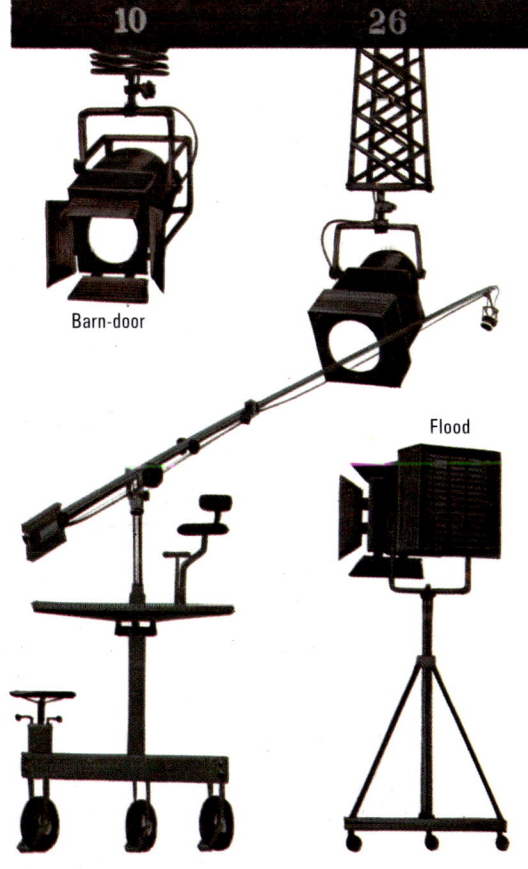

Title captions are done in a number of ways. One caption machine has long wooden blocks which can be rotated, another is simply a rotating drum, and another is a wide moving belt. For quick captions, a special typewriter is used, with the words coming up electrically, and superimposed on the screen.

Various types of lamps are used to light the scene. Spotlights are for lighting small areas, floods for big ones. 'Barn-door' lights have flaps which can be adjusted. The lamps arc up to 10 kilowatts in power, and are suspended from above, either from cables or rods. The amount of power used for big scenes is tremendous, and we can imagine the heat when as many as a thousand lights are all in use.

Television by Satellite

Television signals can be received on sets only for a limited distance from the transmitter. For long distances, other ways must be found to 'boost' the power of the signal. For very long distances, a communications satellite is used: the first and most famous one was *Telstar*.

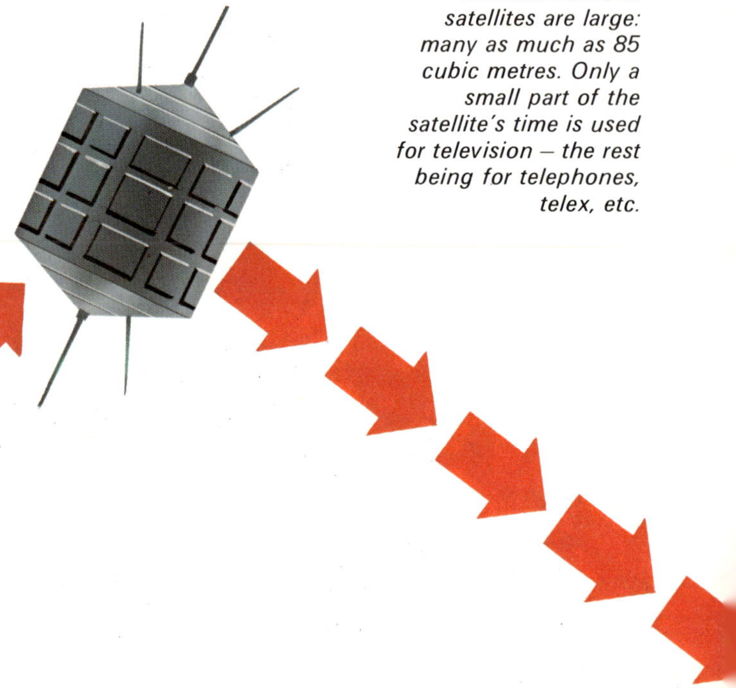

Communications satellites are large: many as much as 85 cubic metres. Only a small part of the satellite's time is used for television — the rest being for telephones, telex, etc.

A whole range of very large communications satellites now orbit the earth, which make it possible for television pictures to be sent and received from many parts of the earth. Satellites take their power from the sun, storing the power in batteries aboard. If a programme is to be sent from, say, the U.S.A. to Europe, the signals are 'beamed up' to the satellite, which in turn, transmits the signals back to earth at an angle which hits the receiving station in Europe. The signals received do not have much power, so a large, dish-shaped aerial is necessary at the receiving end. From here, the signals are sent out to the television studio.

The Story of Television

Above: The first transatlantic television. Mrs Howe, in London, was seen on a TV screen in New York.

Who invented television? As with so many other modern discoveries, television is the result of the work of a number of people. Perhaps the first step was the 'writing telegraph' invented by Bakewell in the middle of the 19th century. The beginning of the photo-electric cell came with the work of Louis May and Willoughby Smith in 1873, and the discovery of the cathode-ray tube by Sir William Crookes in 1878. A year earlier, the French inventor Senleq produced his 'Telectroscope', which 'drew' a picture electrically on to a glass screen. A nearer approach to television was the 'electric vision' system invented in 1880 by the Englishmen Ayrton and Perry. This converted a picture, by means of photo-electric cells, into electricity. One very important step was the mechanical scanning disc invented in 1884 by the Polish scientist, Paul Nipkow. Such a disc was used by John Logie Baird, the British inventor, when he made his first experimental transmission in 1926. His system was taken up by the BBC, and was used by them in the first regular television programme in the world in 1932. The BBC later adopted an electronic scanning system invented by Vladimir Zworykin in the United States.

One of the problems of sending a television programme by satellite is that different TV systems are used in the various countries. Most European countries use the 625-line standard, but North America and Japan use 525 lines. Apart from this, the 625 standard transmits 25 pictures per second, while the 525 system sends 30. This means that, before the pictures can be screened, the picture must be converted from one line-standard to the other electronically.

Below: John Logie Baird with an early transmitting system based on the Nipkow Disc. The disc is punched with a spiral of holes and is scanned by a light which shines through the revolving holes of the disc. The apparatus is made of an amazing jumble of cardboard, string and second-hand bits and pieces, but it worked, and was to become the first successful television transmitter.

GLOSSARY OF TERMS

AERIAL a metal rod or wire used for picking up a radio signal
AMPLIFIER an apparatus for strengthening an electric signal
AUDIO used to describe sound in connection with electronic apparatus
CAMERA TUBE found in a television camera, and on which the visual image forms
CATHODE RAY TUBE a kind of valve used in a television set on the end of which the picture appears
CHANNEL a band of radio frequencies
ELECTRON a very small particle in the atom, charged negatively
ELECTRON GUN the part of a cathode-ray tube which fires a stream of electrons
FREQUENCY The number of radio waves per second
IMAGE ORTHICON TUBE television camera tube which converts an optical image into a varying electric current
MAGNETIC TAPE a length of tape, made of plastic, and coated with particles. When magnetized, these make a record of the signal sent, and the tape reproduces the signal when played back
MONITOR picture tube used for checking the vision signal
PHOTO-ELECTRIC CELL device that converts light into electrical impulses

The greatest feat ever performed by television satellite was when the American space team Armstrong and Aldrin walked on the moon, and the event was televised worldwide.

PHOSPHOR used to coat the inside of a television tube
RADIO WAVE radiated waves of electromagnetic energy
SCANNING movement of a light beam or beam of electrons across a picture in a series of lines
SHADOW SCREEN perforated metal plate used for aligning the colour electron beams in a cathode-ray tube
TELECINE machine for showing cinema films on television
VIDEO-TAPE RECORDER machine for recording television pictures on magnetic tape
WAVELENGTH the length of one complete radio wave
ZOOM LENS a camera lens which can take long-shots or close-ups on the same camera

KEY DATES

1847 'Facsimile transmitter' invented by Bakewell.
1873 Photo-electric effect on selenium discovered by May.
1877 'Telectroscope' invented by Senleq.
1884 Rotating disc scanner invented by Nipkow.
1897 First cathode-ray tube invented by Karl Ferdinand Braun.
1901 Guglielmo Marconi, inventor of wireless telegraphy, sends the letter "S" across the Atlantic.
1907 Rotating mirror scanner invented by Boris Rosing.
1908 A. A. Campbell-Swinton experiments with cathode-ray tubes as television receivers.
1923 John Logie Baird's first television experiments.
1923 'Iconoscope' television camera tube invented by Zworykin.
1929 First all-electric television produced in U.S.A.
1930 First simultaneous sound-and-vision transmission by BBC.
1930 Radio Corporation of America make experimental transmissions.
1932 BBC begin regular transmissions.
1932 Germany begins television transmissions (mechanical scanning).
1936 All-electric television transmissions begun by BBC.
1936 EMI introduce their 'Emiscope' electronic television tube.
1939 Electronic television transmissions start in U.S.A.
1940 Mechanical colour television demonstrated by Goldmark.
1956 First all-colour television station opens in Chicago, U.S.A.
1957 British colour television system demonstrated.
1960 Colour television transmissions begin in Japan.
1962 First television transmission by satellite via Telstar.
1967 Colour television transmissions begin in Britain, France, West Germany and U.S.S.R.

OTHER BOOKS TO READ

About Anglia The Boydell Press, Ipswich.
Basic Television by H. A. Cole. The Technical Press.
Radio & Television (Macdonald Junior Ref. Lib.) Macdonald Educational.
Television by Keith Wicks. Macdonald Educational.
Television – Behind the Screen by P. Fairley. Independent Television Publications Ltd.
Television (Everyday Technology Series) by J. O. E. Clark. Dent.
Television – The First Forty Years by A. Davis. Independent Television Publications Ltd.
Television – Here is the News by A. Davis. Independent Television Publications Ltd.

INDEX

A
actor 9, 16, 18, 24
Armstrong and Aldrin 28
autocue 20
Ayrton 27

B
back-projection 25
Baird, John Logie 7, 27, 28
Bakewell 27
'barn-door' lights 4, 24

C
cable 7, 20, 22
camera 8, 11, 12, 14, 15, 17, 18, 20, 22, 25
camera tube 12, 28
captions 14, 20, 23, 24
carpenter 8, 18
cartoons 19
casting director 16, 18
cathode ray tube 14, 28
children's television 19
colour 11, 12, 28
commentator 22
commercials 19
control room 7, 9, 11, 17, 22
costume 8, 16, 18
Crookes, Sir William 27

D
designer 16, 18
dichroic mirror 12
director 8, 11, 16, 17, 18, 19
'dollies' 12

E
editing 8, 9, 15, 19
editor 16, 20
electron gun 12, 28

F
film 9, 14, 16, 19, 20, 22, 25
'flashed' 9
floor manager 8, 17
flying-spot prism telecine 14
frequency 13, 28

G
graphics 8

H
Hertz 13
'hook-up' 9

L
land line 9
lens 8, 12, 23, 28
lighting 4, 8, 11, 17, 22, 24
line-standard 13, 27
location 7, 19

M
make-up 8
May, Louis 27
microphone 8, 11, 12, 17, 23
mobile studio 22
monitor screen 9, 11, 17, 20, 22, 23, 28

N
network 9
news 8, 9, 20
Nipkow disc 27, 28

O
outside broadcast 9, 20, 22, 23

P
Perry 27
photo-electric cell 14, 27, 28
playback head 14, 15
producer 8, 16, 18, 22
production assistant 11
programme researcher 8
projector 14

prompt book 22
prompter 9
'props' 8, 17, 24, 25

R
recording 8, 9, 14, 15

S
satellite 20, 26, 28
scan 13, 14, 27, 28
'scanner' 23, 28
screen 8, 13, 27
script 9, 11, 16, 18, 20
Senleq 27, 28
set 8, 16, 18, 24
'shadow' plate 13, 28
Smith, Willoughby 27
sound control 7, 8, 11, 22
sound track 14

T
tape 8, 15
technical liaison manager 11
telecine 9, 11, 14, 28
'Telectroscope' 27, 28
Telstar 26, 28
transmission 7, 9, 11, 20, 28
transmitter 7, 13, 26, 27, 28

V
V.H.F. radio 9
video-tape 7, 8, 9, 15, 16, 19, 20, 25, 28
vidicon cross-fire machine 14
vision mixer 11
vision operator 11, 22

W
wardrobe department 8, 16, 18
wavelength 13, 28
wind machine 25

Z
'zoom' 12, 23, 28
Zworykin, Vladimir 27, 28

ACKNOWLEDGEMENTS
Photographs: Endpapers BBC; p. 6 Zefa; p. 7 Zefa; p. 27 BBC and Radio Times Hulton Picture Library; p. 28 NASA.